PROPHETIC EVENTS BEING FULFILLED IN THIS GENERATION

DANIEL ROPP

Copyright © 2024 by Daniel Ropp.

ISBN: 979-8-89465-098-2 (sc)
ISBN: 979-8-89465-099-9 (e)

All rights reserved. No part of this publication may be reproduced, distributed, or transmitted in any form or by any means, including photocopying, recording, or other electronic or mechanical methods, without the prior written permission of the author, except in the case of brief quotations embodied in critical reviews and certain other noncommercial uses permitted by copyright law.

Printed in the United States of America.

Integrity Publishing
39343 Harbor Hills Blvd Lady Lake, FL 32159

www.integrity-publishing.com

CONTENTS

Chapter One: Discovering the Prophetic................. 1
Chapter Two: Progression of Prophetic Destiny............ 8
Chapter Three: God Has His Appointed Times.......... 13
Chapter Four: How Long After The Rapture Until
          The Seven Year Tribulation Begins......... 19
Chapter Five: Unfolding Mystery and the Apostasia....... 25
Chapter Six: End of the Age – End of the World.......... 33
Chapter Seven: What Do You Do With Truth?.......... 41
Chapter Eight: Resurrection of Life and Restoration....... 50
Chapter Nine: The Ten Horns and the Last Trumpet...... 56
Chapter Ten: Revealing Two Mysteries................. 60
Chapter Eleven: America In Prophecy.................. 64
Chapter Twelve: Expectant or Unaware and The Temple ... 76
Chapter Thirteen: War of Ezekiel 38 and 39 versus
          Armageddon 84
Chapter Fourteen: Cherished Secret Revealed............ 89
Chapter Fifteen: The Significance of the Two Witnesses.... 92
Chapter Sixteen: Identifying Mystery Babylon, the Great ... 95
Chapter Seventeen: The Abominable Trend of America ... 106
Chapter Eighteen: The New Jerusalem 112
Chapter Nineteen: The First and Second Creation 115
Chapter Twenty: Amazing Encounters 118
Chapter Twenty-One: A Proper Acknowledgement....... 124

INTRODUCTION

The prophetic events, the mysteries of Bible prophecy that will be addressed, will focus mainly on the generation that began in 1948 up to our present time. The accurate fulfillment of Bible prophecy is what makes the Bible unique from all other books. Our generation is unique in that it is a generation that is now being subjected to end-time events.

If a person reads the Bible from cover to cover they will discover there is one overriding theme and it centers around one person and eventually reveals that person to be Jesus Christ. In the last book of the Bible, Revelation chapter 19 and verse 10, an angel says that the testimony of Jesus is the spirit of prophecy. So you would think that the prophetic theme would be addressed as a priority in the Church in the end time, but sadly, in so many churches this is not the case.

The real reason why Christians around the world are persecuted and the Bible banned is that enemies of God are afraid the remaining prophecies, it speaks of, might be true because so many former prophecies turned out to be true. The Bible reveals that in the end-time Christ will return as King of kings to rule the world and His rule is to never end. To keep this from happening, the powers that be know that Israel must exist when Christ returns or it will nullify all prophecy concerning the establishment of Christ's kingdom. This is why intolerant nations keep trying to wipe Israel off the map. Oh, this quest to know truth is just beginning.

Yes, this generation is a unique generation from all others, and it is through Bible prophecy that we know about it. The Lord is very gracious to inform us through His word that there is a flood event on the horizon, a flood of evil that will increase and pervade society. There will also be an ark of safety event that will precede it by way of the catching out of the Church. More on this later. Hopefully, we will see the need to take the prophetic entreaties seriously.

Scriptures for these prophecies will be quoted from NASV, and Septuagint where additional clarification can be found but the primary quotes will be from the New King James Version.

CHAPTER ONE

Discovering the Prophetic

The end time? Unbelievers typically believe that things will continue on in the same way, but down inside they are somewhat challenged to believe this. Why? Because the events they see happening around them and around the world aren't so ordinary anymore. The events would be more truthfully described as unusual, record breaking or extraordinary. Also, within our country we now have a president who has no qualms about disregarding our Constitution by using his executive orders, downsizing our military and purging it of anything Christian that he can. Free speech is being replaced with political correctness. Yes, we would have to say he gave us change but that change is not normal; it is abnormal. The outcomes we see are not favorable when they take away from us the liberties that we had in the past. The promise of better times is really elusive at best.

The Christian who understands Bible prophecy would say these things are to be expected because we are living in the end time. Christians have available to them insight into the end of the age from the writings of the prophets, from Jesus and the apostles, the early Church fathers, and the Holy Spirit who tells us things to come (John 16.13). Using the time frame given to us <u>from the Bible</u> we know human life began on this planet a little over 6,000 years ago. Some might be surprised as to what the early Church fathers believed in this regard. Irenaeus was one of them who lived 120-202 A.D. He said, "For in as many days as this world was made in so many thousand years shall it be concluded. For the day of the Lord is as a thousand years; and in six days created things were completed: it is evident therefore, that they will come to an end at the six thousandth year." [from Irenaeus chap. XXVII book V]

What he surmised was not a prophetic word from the Lord but this is what he believed. What is interesting is that the generation we are now living in is the period of the end Irenaeus spoke of, so he would say that we are living in the end-time. He said that people will be spiritually blind, not acknowledging the truth, in the depths of ignorance and as wastewater from a sink. Then he makes a crowning statement, "...And therefore, when in the end the Church shall be suddenly caught up from this, it is said, 'there shall be tribulation such as not been since the beginning, neither shall be.'" [Irenaeus chapter XXIX book V]

So we will let Irenaeus be a documented witness that we are living in the time of the end. Because of hindsight, we can see now where God gave a very specific clue as to **when** the end-time generation would commence. The clue He linked to Israel who would become His time clock for the rest of the world. The first clue to us, began with the birth of Abram and he would become the father of the Hebrew people. So, what was the clue? It was the year of his birth which was precisely 1948 years after Adam. One might think – ah, but that is just a coincidence. But was it really?

Notice what God said about Himself in the book of Isaiah chapter 46 verse 9b-10a. "...I am God and there is none like Me declaring the end from the beginning..." In this case, the beginning plan for the nation of Israel began with the birth of Abram.

It took Jesus to help us understand the clue to make sense of the timing. Jesus gave us the most profound insight with the parable of the fig tree. The fig tree, in scripture, represents the state of Israel. So, the parable indicated that when the fig tree (Israel) emerged from its dormant state, (this implied it would be recognized again as the state of Israel), it would signal the time period of the last generation in which Jesus would return to earth and set up His kingdom to rule upon the earth for 1,000 years. The first part of this parable(and prophecy) has been fulfilled when Israel was declared an independent state May 14, **1948**. In the parable, Jesus also said that it would be summer when it happened and the month of May is when summer starts in Israel and their independence was also declared on the very day of the Festival of the Fig Tree. Even the details of His prophecy were fulfilled.

Jesus went on to speak about the events that would take place in the 1948 generation in the book of Matthew chapter 24. He makes a crucial statement in verse 34. He said, "Assuredly, I say to you this generation will by no means pass away til all these things take place." So, Jesus is saying **this generation** will see the consummation of all these things affirming that those living in this 1948 generation are living in the end – time!

The prophet Hosea, who lived about 785 B.C., spoke of this. In Hosea 6.1-2, speaking about Israel, he says "Come and let us return to the Lord; for He has torn, but He will heal us; He has stricken but He will bind us up. After two days He will revive us; on the third day He will raise us up that we may live in His sight." In decoding his prophecy, you realize that each of these days represents a thousand years where it says, "after two days He will revive us."

With regard to this prophecy, when was Israel "torn" and "stricken?" It was in 63 B.C. when the Romans came into Israel and conquered it. That was the starting point for this prophecy. And when was Israel revived? They were revived in 1948 A.D. when they emerged from a dormant state after 2,000 years. The prophecy said it would be after two days or two thousand years. Was it? Yes, it was eleven years after!

So this part of the prophecy has been fulfilled in our 1948 generation.

You see, in this prophecy the promise is made to the generation of Israel, now revived, that they will "live in His sight" on the third day. The second prophetic day has passed and the third day has begun. Yes, this 1948 generation has extended right into the third day and it is the generation that will visibly see Jesus return as King to the earth after which Israel is promised a spiritual restoration.

Yes, we can document that the prophet Hosea identifies the 1948 generation as the end-time generation. From the evidence that we have, it is apparent that the destiny of many hangs on whether one believes in the fulfillment of Bible prophecy or not. Bible prophecy, for the end-time, does not end here as we go on. The evidence only becomes more compelling.

God knows exactly what He is doing. Satan and the secular world do not want to believe they have lost their war against God. So, the battles for the souls of men continue. In some respects, it would seem that Satan has the upper hand. Most of the secular learning institutions exclude God from the learning process any way they can. Don't think that's true? Try teaching Creation Science in the classroom and see what happens. Try teaching that abortion is wrong and see what happens. I think I have made my point without needing to make a long list.

So, what we have in society now is an on-going downward trend away from the things of God. In fact, this trend would become so significant that it was prophesied in the Bible to happen in the latter days. In the book of 1 Timothy chapter four and verses 1-2 this declaration is made, "Now the Spirit expressly says that in the latter times some will depart from the faith, giving heed to deceiving spirits and doctrines of demons speaking lies in hypocrisy having their own conscience seared with a hot iron.

In the book of 2 Timothy chapter three verses 1-4 it says, "But know this that <u>in the last days</u> perilous times will come;

for men will be lovers of themselves, lovers of money, boasters, proud, blasphemers, disobedient to parents, unthankful, unholy, unloving, unforgiving, slanderers without self-control, brutal, despisers of good, traitors, headstrong, haughty, lovers of pleasure rather than lovers of God." This describes our present day society to a T. Therefore, we indeed must be living in the last days prophetic time period. So, none of this has caught God by surprise. It was prophesied in His word around 1900 years ago. These signs are a final warning of what is yet to come.

What emerges on the world scene in such a time as this is the antichrist. The Muslims call him their Mahdi and the apostle Paul identifies him as the man of sin. Second Thessalonians 2.9-12 reads, "The coming of the lawless one is according to the working of Satan with all power, signs, and lying wonders, and with all unrighteous deception among those who perish, because they did not receive the love of the truth that they might be saved. And for this reason, God will send them strong delusion that they should believe the lie, that they all may be condemned who did not believe the truth but had pleasure in unrighteousness."

Yes, the antichrist will emerge to rule the world during the great tribulation time and Jesus identified that this would occur in the generation in which Israel would become an independent state once again. In Matthew 24.34 He said, "... this generation will by no means pass away till all these things take place." Jesus listed a number of things that would take place (Matthew 24.15-30) in this generation, and two very significant events were the great tribulation and His coming back to earth in power and great glory. What should get our attention is that over 76 years of this generation He spoke of have already gone by!

In Matthew 24.37-39, Jesus also prophesied to say, "But as the days of Noah were so also will the coming of the Son of Man be. For as in the days before the flood they were eating and drinking, marrying and giving in marriage, until the day that Noah entered the ark, and did not know until the flood came and took them all away, so also will the coming of the Son of Man be."

So how was it in the days of Noah before the flood? Well the people in Noah's day did not believe Noah's message of warning was relevant to them so they dismissed it out of hand. Wouldn't you agree the same thing is happening today fulfilling Jesus' prophecy?

The man of sin is about to emerge on the world stage and society has two choices; to align themselves with Christ or with the antichrist. Christ does not force anyone to accept Him as their Savior. He simply entreats you while the Age of Grace is still in your favor. The antichrist, on the other hand, will through his false prophet, force society to worship him. In Revelation 13.15-17 it says, "He was granted power to give breath to the image of the beast, that the image of the beast should both speak and cause as many as would not worship the image of the beast to be killed. He causes all both small and great, rich and poor, free and slave, to receive a mark on their right hand or on their foreheads, and that no one may buy or sell except one who has the mark or the name of the beast, or the number of his name."

If you are wondering how those are killed who don't comply it is through decapitation (Revelation 20.4) the very thing ISIS has done in the middle east. ISIS is one group of people known as the Mahdi's people – the antichrist's people. Do you see the handwriting on the wall yet?

The World Health Organization has used the covid-19 pandemic as a beta test for compliance. You may be wondering how this has anything to do with scripture? The WHO solution for the supposed virus was for everyone to be inoculated with a vaccine. There were red flags from the very beginning. It was touted that the vaccine was safe but if it was safe then why were people threatened to take it for a disease supposedly so deadly that you needed to be tested to even know if you have it? Why were other **remedies forbidden** to be used, such as Ivermectin, in place of getting the vaccination? It turns out the vaccine did not keep one from getting covid-19. If we get back to the scripture we will see where it exposes this great deception and it is found in Revelation chapter 18.

Revelation chapter 18 alludes to the greatest center of world commerce, how great it had become, and then to its fall from greatness. What is interesting is verse 23. It reads, "For your merchants were the great men of the earth, for by your sorcery all the nations were deceived." There are two things here that are very noteworthy. First, is the word "sorcery" and the Greek word is actually pharmakeia from which our word pharmacy comes from. Guess what? It has been the pharmacy corporations that have generated the vaccines for the Corona virus and those vaccines have been mandated by most nations of the whole world to supposedly combat the virus. The nation's leaders fell right in lockstep to mandate these vaccines. Did you notice, the verse of scripture said that because of this the nations were **deceived!** The second thing to make note of, is this chapter is being represented in the time period of the tribulation. This means this deception will continue right into the tribulation period from where we are right now.

God is allowing this tine of trial for the world because the world has largely rejected Him. But as in the days of Noah there was an ark of safety but one had to get into it to be safe. That ark today is Jesus Christ. If one repents of their sins and accepts Christ as their Savior and Lord they will be raptured out and escape the horrible period of the tribulation. But if one hasn't made the all-important decision there isn't much time left in which to make that choice.

CHAPTER TWO

PROGRESSION OF PROPHETIC DESTINY

In the book of Mark chapter one verses 14-15 it says, "...Jesus came into Galilee preaching the gospel of God, and saying, "The time is fulfilled, and the kingdom of God is at hand; repent and believe in the gospel."' So, the message of the kingdom of God was a message for people to repent and turn to God. As a result, a person entering into the kingdom of God enters into a new freedom having their sins forgiven, and the benefit of that is knowing the righteousness of Christ, His joy, and peace in the Holy Spirit (Romans 14.17).

This was a concept that the religious sects of the day did not understand. In the book of Luke chapter 17 and verses 20-21 it says, "Now having been questioned by the Pharisees as to when the kingdom of God was coming, He answered them and said, "The kingdom of God is not coming with signs to be observed; nor will they say, "Look here it is!" For behold, the kingdom of God is in your midst." The New King James version says that the kingdom of God is within you, but the NASV says the kingdom of God is in your midst and is more accurately rendered as we will see.

Jesus was exercising the power and authority of His kingship right in their midst yet they didn't realize what was happening. They didn't recognize they were opposing the works of the kingdom of God.

Jesus went on to say, in the following verses, that the days would come when He wouldn't be among them and terrible times would come after (verses 26-29). But He also indicated that before judgments will fall upon the world there will be an exception (vv.30-36). First, in verse 34 He says, "I tell you on that night there will be two in one bed; one will be taken and the other left. (v35) There will be two women grinding at the same place; one will be taken and the other left. (v.36) Two men will be in the field; one will be taken and the other left."

In Tyndale's version (1534 A.D.) he translated the verse to read "…one will be received and the other will be forsaken," in each case. This clearly reveals Jesus was referring to a catching away of the saints and those forsaken would be left to face judgments that will likely bring death to many of them.

So, an unbeliever should really ask themselves why would I not want to enter into the kingdom of God since it will turn out to be very unprofitable not to? Since this is now the generation of the Lord's return no one can afford to miss this **appointed time!**

Let's look at major turning points in time. As you know, the first major turning point came when Adam and Eve sinned by disobeying God in the garden of Eden. Adamic sin was perpetuated from that point onward. In fact, it became such a major problem that God had to destroy the world by a flood which was the second major turning point in man's history.

The third major turning point came when God confused the languages of the people at the tower of Babel. But Genesis 10.25 goes on to say something very interesting. "To Eber were born two sons; the name of one was Peleg for in his days the earth was divided…" It doesn't say the people were divided but the earth and seems to indicate when the continents were separated from each other.

The fourth major turning point came when God decided to set aside a people for Himself through whom the nations would be blessed. It began with the birth of Abram 1948 years after Adam. In Genesis 22.18 God speaking to Abraham said, "In your seed all the nations of the earth shall be blessed, because you have obeyed My voice."

The fifth major turning point came with the birth of Jacob. In Genesis 28.13-14 God spoke to Jacob in a dream and said, "I am the Lord God of Abraham, your father and the God of Isaac; the land on which you lie I will give to you and your descendants. Also, your descendants shall be as the dust of the earth... and in you and in your seed all the families of the earth shall be blessed." Some years later God changed Jacob's name to Israel (Genesis 32.28). A few more years go by and God tells Israel to go to Egypt and he would make of him a great nation there (Genesis 46.2-4).

The sixth major turning point came when Israel departed Egypt under Moses. Exodus 12.40-41 reads, "Now the sojourn of the children of Israel who lived in Egypt was four hundred and thirty years – on that very same day – it came to pass that all the armies of the Lord went out from the land of Egypt." Then 40 years later they entered the land of promise and claimed it as the land of Israel.

The seventh major turning point came with the birth of king David. In 2 Samuel 7.16 the following is said concerning the Davidic kingdom: "And your house and your kingdom shall be established forever before you. Your throne shall be established forever." This was important because for this to happen the Messiah would have to come through the line of David, which He did. Matthew 1.1 says, "The book of the genealogy of Jesus Christ, the son of David, the son of Abraham."

The eighth major turning point came with the birth of Jesus Christ. Yes, He was born in the land that was promised to Abraham, Isaac, and Jacob. He completed, by fulfilling the first phase of His coming in being the sinless sacrifice to redeem the fallen race. This was huge! He revealed His deity by all the miracles that He did. Even the prophecies that He made are still being fulfilled to our present day. More on that later.

The ninth major turning point came with the birth of the Church after Jesus ascended into heaven. This initiated evangelism to the entire world to build Christ's kingdom.

The tenth major turning point happened in May of 1948 when Israel became an independent state once again fulfilling Jesus' prophecy in the parable of the fig tree. The reason it is so significant, is Jesus indicated once that happened, it signaled the generation that would conclude the age, and this same generation will embrace the next three major turning points.

The eleventh major turning point will be when the rapture of the Church occurs and it is to happen in this generation we are living in now!

The twelfth major turning point will happen six months later when the two witnesses come to Israel and in 3 ½ years they will have 144,000 converts added to Christ's kingdom.

The thirteenth major turning point will happen one month after the two witnesses come to Israel and the antichrist emerges on the inter-national world scene and is given authority to rule over the nations and he will rule for seven tumultuous years.

The fourteenth major turning point will happen when Jesus returns with millions of His saints (yes, in this generation) to set up His earthly kingdom and He will rule the world for 1,000 years.

Here's the rub. The antichrist and all those supporting him will think they have totally triumphed over Jesus Christ's followers only to be greatly surprised in the end when they see Jesus returning to over- throw all rebellion against God. This begins the judgment of nations (Matthew 25.31-46). Now the tables are turned and all the unjust and evil will be purged from Christ's kingdom and thrown into the lake of fire. Yes, anyone who was an accessory to the antichrist's objectives in supporting eradication of just people **will be purged from His kingdom and thrown into the lake of fire!** If this isn't a sobering thought I don't know what is. The human race has been warned by Jesus what He will do when He comes back as the King of kings. He won't be a pansy or a pacifist. He will be a Leader of leaders, a Lord of lords! Yes, it is decision time.

Revelation 22.10-11 states, "...the time is at hand. He who is unjust, let him be unjust still; he who is filthy, let him be filthy still; he who is righteous, let him be righteous still; he who is holy, let him be holy still." Jesus is indicating that by the choice we make we will have to live with the consequences of that choice!

In the next chapter we will see the significance of God's appointed times.

CHAPTER THREE

GOD HAS HIS APPOINTED TIMES

There are future events that have their appointed times **designated by God.** In the book of Isaiah chapter 44.6-7 we read, "Thus says the Lord, the King of Israel, and His Redeemer, the Lord of hosts; 'I am the First and I am the Last; besides Me there is no God. And who can proclaim as I do? Then let him declare it and set it in order for Me. Since I appointed the ancient people, and the things that are coming and shall come.'"

God makes it clear there are future events that have their appointed times or set times. God never says, oops I missed that one. No, He is always right on time. An example from Exodus 12.40-41 reads, "Now the sojourn of the children of Israel who lived in Egypt was 430 years. And it came to pass at the end of the four hundred and thirty years – on that very same day – it came to pass that all the armies of the Lord went out from the land of Egypt.

Another example is found in Leviticus 23. 4-5. It reads, "These are the feasts of the Lord, holy convocations which you shall proclaim at their appointed times. On the fourteenth day of the first month at twilight is the Lord's Passover." So, this appointed time was fulfilled when? Exactly on the day Jesus was crucified. Matthew 26.17-18 reads, "Now on the first day of the Feast of Unleavened Bread the disciples came to Jesus saying to Him, 'where do you want us to prepare for You to eat the Passover?' And He said, 'Go into the city to a certain man, and say to him, 'the Teacher says, My <u>time is at hand</u>; I will keep the Passover at your house with My disciples.'"

Did you notice what Jesus said? He said, "My time is at hand." Jesus was referring to the <u>appointed time</u> set by God previously that we read about in Leviticus. Yes, Jesus was the Passover sacrifice and He fulfilled it to the very day!

In the book of Daniel, Gabriel reveals to Daniel that there is an <u>appointed time</u> for the indignation, that is, God's wrath. Daniel 8.19 reads, "...Look, I am making known to you what shall happen in the latter time of the indignation; for at the <u>appointed time</u> the end shall be."

It was also revealed to Daniel that the actions of the antichrist, in the end time, against the Jews would come to an end. Daniel 8.31 and 35 says, "And forces shall be mustered by him, and they shall defile the sanctuary fortress; then they shall take away the daily sacrifice and place there the abomination of desolation. [v35] And some of those of understanding shall fall, to refine them, purify them, and make them white until the time of the end; because it is still for the <u>appointed time</u>."

The prophet Habakkuk was frustrated and dismayed that the wicked were getting by with so much violence and there seemed to be no justice. The vision he had sounds so much like what ISIS was getting by with. God speaks to Habakkuk in chapter two and verse three. He says, "For the vision is yet for an <u>appointed time</u>; but in the end it will speak, and it will not lie..." Then in chapter three verses 12-13 it reveals what happens at the appointed time. "You marched through the land in indignation; You trampled nations in anger. You went forth for the salvation of Your people, for salvation with Your anointed. You struck the head from the house of the wicked..." This is exactly what it is talking about in Revelation 19.14-15 when Jesus comes back with the armies of heaven at the end of the great tribulation time.

The Egyptian Pharoah was a type of the antichrist. When dealing with Moses he was a deceiver and a liar. It is interesting after God's people were delivered out of Egypt that God destroyed not only Pharaoh but the entire Egyptian army. And so it will be at the end of the age that the antichrist will be destroyed and his army by none other than Jesus Christ who previously delivered His people out of the world.

The rapture is yet another <u>appointed time</u> soon to be fulfilled. It is found in the book of Departure, also known as the book of Exodus chapter 23 and verse 15. It reads, "You shall keep the Feast of Unleavened Bread (you shall eat unleavened bread seven days as I commanded you, at the time <u>appointed</u> in the month Abib, for in it you came out of Egypt; none shall appear before Me empty handed)." It is interesting that the rapture, that is, a translation of God's saints confirms a departure.

In the book of Deuteronomy 16.3 Moses repeats God's command by saying, "...seven days you shall eat unleavened bread with it, that is the bread of affliction (for you came out of Egypt in haste...)"

Did you notice the words "bread of affliction?" That word "affliction" in the Hebrew can also mean "tribulation." If you go back over 400 years to when the latest edition of the Geneva Bible was written it uses that exact word "tribulation." So, concerning the Feast of Unleavened Bread we see a component that it is associated with – a time of trouble (tribulation). According to verse three they were to eat the bread of tribulation for seven days to remember <u>the day in which they came out</u>. The time period of seven days is a type of the seven years of the tribulation period; but they were to remember that **they were delivered from it!**

We know keeping the Feast of Unleavened Bread represented the very moment of departure from Egypt, the land of bondage, a type of the world, therefore the fulfilment of this <u>appointed time</u> represents the departing of the children of God from the world through the rapture. But did you notice the last part of verse 15? It said, "...none shall appear before Me empty-handed."

Guess where the Church, the people of God, are taken at the time of the rapture? First Thessalonians 3.13 says, "so that He may establish your hearts blameless in holiness <u>before our God and Father at the coming of our Lord Jesus Christ with all His saints</u>." So, we come into the presence of God just as it was expected under the Feast of Unleavened Bread in the Exodus account.

The fulfillment of the Feast of Unleavened Bread goes even further, as in the Exodus account none of God's people were to appear before Him empty-handed. The answer or fulfillment of this is found in Revelation 22.12. It says, "And behold I am coming quickly <u>and My reward is with Me, to give to everyone</u> according to his work." We won't be empty-handed. We will have our rewards.

I believe this is the next <u>appointed time</u> on God's calendar! When the rapture occurs, it will constitute the greatest deliverance in the history of mankind outside of the cross. God told Moses this was to be remembered forever. This appointed time will affect every one of us one way or another. The removal of hundreds of millions of people from the earth quickly, all at the same time, will disrupt economies worldwide. Christians are faithful to pay their bills and their taxes. When this stream of revenue dries up to counties, states and governments it will be very problematic. Workers performing jobs will suddenly not be there to do the work companies were counting on them to do. Many farmers won't be here to harvest or plant crops. It will undoubtably take a few months to sort things out before the antichrist appears. Supply chain shortages will be a nightmare, and things will only get much worse with the quickly approaching seven-year tribulation period.

Mentioned previously were several things on God's appointed time schedule from Leviticus chapter 23. Two of those events were the Passover and the Feast of Unleavened Bread. The Feast of Unleavened Bread was to be kept for seven days not just the evening of the Passover, and it was observed <u>at the departure</u> of God's people from Egypt.

Having reviewed these things, we go to an interesting statement made by Jesus, Himself, at the time He kept the last Passover with His disciples. The words of Jesus are found in Luke 22.15-16. He said, "With fervent desire I have desired to eat this Passover with you before I suffer; for I say to you, I will no longer eat of it **until it is fulfilled in the kingdom of God.**"

It would only be a matter of a few hours and Jesus would be fulfilling His role as the Passover Sacrifice so what still needed to be fulfilled in the kingdom of God? Answer – it was the Feast of Unleavened Bread, and it would be fulfilled where? Answer – in the kingdom of God!

We find in the book of Daniel chapter seven verses 13-14 that the time comes when Jesus is brought before the Father and the kingdom that was promised to Him is finally given to Him. The timing this occurs is revealed to us in Revelation 11.15, after the sounding of the seventh trumpet.

So the fulfillment of the Feast of Unleavened Bread is finalized in heaven! This feast was directly associated with the departure of God's people and the fulfillment of that type places God's people in heaven because Jesus said that it would be fulfilled in the kingdom of God. The on-going fulfillment of the feast was to last for seven days which is symbolical of the seven years the saints will be in heaven before returning with Christ to rule and reign with Him.

The Church cannot fulfill this without them being translated, so again, this shows there <u>will be</u> a rapture of the saints. Was God's people departing from Egypt a normal departure or was it God assisted? Even Moses said to the people that they had been borne on eagles wings (Exodus 19.4).

The Septuagint emphasizes this point more clearly. Exodus 19.3-4 reads: "And Moses went onto the mountain of God, and God called him from the mountain, saying, "This is what you shall say to the house of Jacob and report to the sons of Israel: You yourselves have seen what I have done to the Egyptians, and **I took you up as though on eagles wings**, and I brought you to Myself.

Yes, the time of God's people, the Church at the rapture will definitely be God assisted, and very soon now the time of our redemption draws near!

CHAPTER FOUR

How Long After The Rapture Until The Seven Year Tribulation Begins

It begins with a question the disciples asked Jesus in Matthew 24.3. They asked, "…What will be the sign of Your coming…? So Jesus answers their question according to how they asked it, that is<u>, with</u> <u>a sign</u> that will precede His coming, and shows this would occur after the tribulation.

We read His answer in verses 29-30. He said, "Immediately <u>after the tribulation</u> of those days the sun will be darkened, and the moon will not give its light, the stars will fall from heaven, and the powers of the heavens will be shaken. <u>Then the sign</u> of the Son of Man will appear in heaven, and then all the tribes of the earth will mourn, and they will see the Son of Man coming on the clouds of heaven with power and great glory."

We are told, that at the time of this coming, the atmosphere will be dark. So, what is the sign? Simply this, a very bright light piercing the darkness which precedes Jesus' descent with His saints. Second Thessalonians 2.8 confirms this when the apostle Paul said that when Jesus comes back He will destroy the antichrist "…with the brightness of His coming."

Jesus went on, to give the disciples additional information as well, concerning **His coming that would not be preceded by any sign** in Matthew 24.37-44. In these verses Jesus is distinguishing His coming in a different way, i.e., a coming that will take people by surprise.

Jesus continues to say, "But as the days of Noah were so also will the coming of the Son of Man be. For as in the days before the flood they were eating and drinking, marrying and giving in marriage, until the day that Noah entered the ark, and did not know until the flood came and took them all away, so also will the coming of the Son of Man be. Then two men will be in the field, one will be taken and the other left. Two women will be grinding at the mill, one will be taken and the other left."

The surprise element here depicts a pretrib rapture. Did you notice that the believer and the unbeliever were openly working side by side here which would be very unlikely if this were the end of a tribulation event. Mass slaughter of tribulation saints is happening in the last 3 ½ years of the tribulation (Daniel 7.25) so any saints who want to continue living at that time would have gone underground and into hiding. They wouldn't be holding down public jobs since the mark of the beast would prevent them from buying or selling. So these working openly are depicting a pretrib environment, one in which a pretrib rapture occurs.

Scripture abounds with clues to a coming translation of the saints. Consider an interesting verse from Malachi 3.17. It reads, "They shall be mine says the Lord of hosts. On the day I make them My jewels. And I will spare them as a man spares his own son who serves him." Now compare the Hebrew phrase "on the day I make them My jewels" to the Greek from the Septuagint which says, "on the day that I make them My acquisition." The word "acquisition" means a rescuing or delivering from in the sense of I've come to collect, gather, or pick up. That is an almost perfect description of a catching away or a rapture event. I find it interesting, that this promise to be spared **precedes** the time of God's wrath as mentioned in the following chapter of Malachi chapter four.

Now to address the question, how long after the rapture until the seven-year tribulation begins? This was a mystery until recently, but to begin to answer this question one of the things we need to know is when is the Festival of Firstfruits? The Festival of Firstfruits is to be celebrated when God's people enter heaven. This will fulfill the type of the Festival of Firstfruits.

Leviticus 23.10-11 puts it this way, "...When you come into the land which I give to you, and reap its harvest, then you shall bring a sheaf of the Firstfruits of your harvest to the priest. He shall wave the sheaf before the Lord, to be accepted on your behalf; <u>on the day after the Sabbath</u> the priest shall wave it." This tells us the Feast of Firstfruits then was to be celebrated on the first day of the week. But what month was it celebrated?

The book of Joshua chapter four, verse 19, tells us <u>when</u> God's people entered the promised land. It reads, "Now the people came up from the Jordan on the tenth day of the first month..." Well, the first month is the month Abib which corresponds to our March/April. Joshua 5.10 goes on to say, "Now the children of Israel camped in Gilgal, and kept the Passover on the 14th day of the month..." So, what followed the Passover (by God's command) was the Feast of Unleavened Bread and then the Feast of Firstfruits all kept in the same month.

To be more precise as to the day in the month Abib that the Feast of Fruits was celebrated, we look at two verses in Leviticus 23.15-16. It reads, "And you shall count for yourselves the day after the Sabbath, from the day that you brought the sheaf of the wave offering; seven sabbaths shall be completed. Count fifty days to the day after the seventh Sabbath; then you shall offer a new grain offering to the Lord." We know the 50-day period as Pentecost. This is celebrated in the month Sivan, which corresponds to our May/June calendar depending on which year it falls in.

So, if you count backwards from Pentecost 50 days you come to the month Abib and the day of the Feast of Firstfruits which is on the first day of the week. This is another way we know Jesus rose on the day of the Feast of Firstfruits as everyone of the gospels says that He rose on the first day of the week.

It is important to remember what the Lord Himself declared concerning the Firstfruits in Leviticus 23.17. He said, "You shall bring from your dwellings two waves loaves… **they** are the Firstfruits to the Lord." Why two? Because there is a Gentile and a Jewish component to the Firstfruits. Jesus previously made provision for the Gentiles when He said in John 10.16, "Other sheep I have which are not of this fold them also I must bring…" There is further evidence of this, on the day of Pentecost, when the disciples found themselves speaking in languages of the Gentiles signifying to the Gentiles that the door was open to them to be included in the Church.

The Church, <u>as the Body of Christ</u>, is declared to be the Firstfruits, and the 144,000 Jews in Revelation 14.4 are also declared to be the Firstfruits to God. This is the only harvest mentioned in the plural (Firstfruits).

In fulfilling the gathering of the harvest, the Church is taken up to the throne of God prior to the start of the tribulation and the 144,000 are taken up at the middle of the seven years of the tribulation. How do we know this is the midpoint of the tribulation for them? Because after they are taken up, the 144,000 are seen standing before the throne of God in heaven in Revelation chapter 14 and we also see an angel warning the inhabitants of the earth not to take the mark of the beast, and this mark was not required by the antichrist until the midpoint of the tribulation.

You see in chapter 13 it is only after the antichrist is given authority to rule for the final 42 months (3 ½ years) that the false prophet causes people to receive the mark (Rev.13.16). One more way we know is in chapter 12 of Revelation, as soon as the man child (144,000 more on this later) is caught up to God's throne the woman (religious Israel) flees into the wilderness where she is fed for <u>the last 1260 days</u> of the tribulation (Rev. 12.6) which represents the last 3 ½ years of that time period.

We now have all the information we need to determine the time lapse after the Church is caught up. First of all, we know the 144,000 are raptured in the month Abib because that is when the Feast of Firstfruits is celebrated and the translation of the 144,000 brings about the <u>final fulfillment</u> for the Feast of Firstfruits. This puts the month of Abib at the end of the first 3 ½ years. So, if you count backwards from the month Abib you come to the starting point for the seven-year tribulation period which turns out to be the Jewish month "Bul." The month "Bul" falls within the Oct/Nov time period on the Gregorian calendar.

I wondered down through the years how long after the rapture of the Church before the antichrist would be revealed. Would it be a matter of days, weeks, months, or what? Now we know. Since the rapture takes place in the month Abib we have a transition period from Abib to Bul. This represents a delay of about seven months.

Transition from one major event to another doesn't happen like turning on a light switch. For example, from the cross to Pentecost there was a 50-day waiting period. So, what might be occurring during the seven-month transition? There is a possibility that Israel may be winding down a war with her enemies because what usually happens when a war concludes is the signing of a peace treaty. Isn't that what we are seeing at the beginning of the seven-year period with the antichrist confirming a covenant of peace with Israel for seven years? (Daniel 9.27)

Now let's see what we find when we try and verify these time periods. Well, we calculated from the midpoint of the tribulation backwards. What do we find if we calculate forward from the mid-point of the seven years to the end of it? Counting forward 3 ½ years you arrive at the month Tishri. What is supposed to happen at the end of the seven years is the Feast of Ingathering which represents **the last of the good harvest.** The Feast of Ingathering occurs in the month Tishri. Exodus 23.16 both describe the Feast of Ingathering as being in the month Tishri which falls within the Sept/Oct period on the Gregorian calendar.

So, now we have a good ball park figure for the length of the transition period which is very comforting because it embraces a sooner departure for the Church than what we may have previously envisioned.

CHAPTER FIVE

Unfolding Mystery and the Apostasia

The book of Daniel speaks of a time of Jacob's trouble and it is fascinating what it reveals. We can view the timing of Jacob's trouble from Jeremiah 30.3-7. It reads, "For behold the days are coming, says the Lord, that I will bring back My people Israel and Judah, says the Lord. And I will cause them to return to the land that I gave their fathers and they shall possess it." Since this has been fulfilled in the 1948 generation, we know we are talking about the last days here.

From verse five, we advance in time to the great tribulation period. Verses 5-7 read, "For thus says the Lord: 'We have heard a voice of trembling, of fear and not of peace. Ask now and see, whether a man is ever in labor with child? So, why do I see every man with his hands on his loins like a woman in labor, and all faces turned pale? Alas! For that day is great so that none is like it; and **it is the time of Jacob's trouble,** but he shall be saved out of it.'"

Did you notice from verse six, only males are being addressed here, and secondly, they are promised not to have to go through the time of Jacob's trouble as they would be saved out of it.

The time is addressed again in the book of Isaiah chapter 66 verses 7-8. It says, "Before she was in labor, she gave birth;

before her pain came <u>she delivered a male child</u>. Who has heard such a thing? Who has seen such things? "Shall the earth be made to give birth in one day? Or shall a nation be born at once? For as soon as Zion was in labor, she gave birth to her children." The word "children" here actually reads as "sons" in the NASV Bible – yes, as males. So, we see here the male child, in the singular, is being represented in the plural as sons.

When you go to Revelation chapter 12 you see a similar scene with the woman and the man child. The setting here is also at the time of Jacob's trouble. Most get the symbolism of verse one correct when they say the woman with the twelve stars represents Israel. But when they get to the male child of verse five, they get it wrong by saying that this represents Jesus. Verse five says, "She bore a male child who was to rule all nations with a rod of iron. And her child was caught up to God and His throne."

First of all, for the child to be Jesus the woman in verse one would have to be represented as Mary, not Israel, but she isn't. Mary has never been portrayed in scripture as being clothed with the sun, the moon under her feet and with a crown of twelve stars.

The next problem we have with the child being Jesus comes from verse four where the dragon stood ready to devour the child as soon as it was born. Yes, there was a threat on Jesus' life by king Herod but it wasn't as soon a Jesus was born but roughly two years later when the wise men arrived from the east to see Him.

The third problem, with this child being Jesus, is that verse five says her child was caught up to God and His throne. Jesus was taken up into heaven after He finished His ministry, but He certainly wasn't a child when it happened. Neither is Jesus taken up into heaven in the middle of the tribulation as this child will be. We know this is the middle of the tribulation because the woman who gives birth flees into the wilderness (v.6) for one thousand two hundred and sixty days which remain of the tribulation time.

So, to be consistent with the way this passage is being interpreted, if the woman, in the singular, represents a plurality of individuals then the man child, in the singular, can also represent a plurality of individuals.

The Old Testament scriptures we looked at previously supports that this is the case. The woman represents the non-Messianic religious Jews who flee into the wilderness. I believe the man-child represents the 144,000 and here is why.

In Revelation chapter eleven we found the two witnesses in Israel witnessing. So, the expected results of their witnessing would be converts, yes, new believers, babes in Christ. And when did the two witnesses finish their ministry? It was finished just before the midpoint of the seven-year tribulation just prior to the man-child being caught up to heaven. Who were their converts, these new believers in Christ? They are the 144,000 represented as the man child, and who are delivered out of Jacob's trouble. All of them are in Israel when they are delivered not scattered throughout the planet witnessing and as we have seen from scripture they are not even on the earth during the last 3 ½ years of the tribulation.

In the book of Daniel 12.1 it mentions that those who are delivered out of the time of Jacob's trouble are those whose names are "found written in the book." We know people's names are written in the Book of Life when they accept Christ as Savior, so if these 144,000 had their names written in the Book of Life prior to the beginning of the tribulation time they would have been part of the Church. Jesus doesn't leave part of the Church behind at the rapture to do more unfinished witnessing. So, this shows the 144,000 were instead converts in the tribulation time.

Revelation chapter 14 verses 4-5 show they are caught up to God and to His throne just like it indicated in Revelation chapter 12 and verse five, and they are also declared to be males as the scripture in the Old Testament said they would be.

The timing fits as well. In chapter 14 they are in heaven just before the proclamation of the angel (vv 9-10) that those on earth are not to take the mark of the beast (and it is not required until the last 3 ½ years of the tribulation).

Return to the woman in Revelation chapter 12 and notice something very interesting about her flight into the wilderness. In verse five it says, "Then the woman fled into the wilderness where she had a place prepared by God..." Then in verse 14 it says, "But the woman was given two wings of a great eagle, that she might fly into the wilderness to her place.

The idea that she is given wings that she might fly would imply there are numerous jumbo jets waiting to take these Jews into the wilderness to safety. Since the antichrist is already in Israel with his army it isn't very likely he would give the airport a pass. On the contrary, he isn't allowing her to escape but rather is trying to prevent it (v.15). So, what we find is another hidden meaning in the statement that she is given two wings. We need to unpack the symbolism.

We find a parallel statement given by God after Israel had come out of Egypt in Exodus 19.4. It reads, You have seen what I did to the Egyptians, and how I bore you on eagles wings and brought you to Myself." They didn't have airplanes back then so we know they didn't fly, but something supernatural did happen and we understand what that was from Isaiah 40.28-29, 31. It reads, "Have you not known? Have you not heard? The everlasting God, the Lord, the Creator of the ends of the earth, neither faints nor is weary. His understanding is unsearchable. He gives power to the weak and to those who have no might He increases strength, but those who wait upon the Lord shall renew their strength; they shall mount up with wings like eagles. They shall run and not be weary, they shall walk and not faint."

How was their departure from Egypt described? Exodus 14.5 says, "Now it was told the king of Egypt that the people had fled..." Another clue revealing the speed at which they traveled was, they weren't even to think about baking any bread with leaven in it for seven days. When you consider the distance they had to travel before crossing the Red Sea it would have required them to travel a minimum of 38 to 40 miles a day – an impossible feat for seven days if you didn't leave anyone behind. But God gave them supernatural strength for seven days to do just that. Pharaoh's army had to use horses and chariots just to catch up.

So, when you see the phrase in Revelation 12.14 that the woman will be given wings as an eagle you know that it likely means, one more time, God is going to supply the woman with supernatural strength to make her escape into the wilderness.

Here is where we run into another interesting parallel. Verse 15 says, "And the serpent poured water like a river out of his mouth after the woman so that he might cause her to be swept away with the flood." So, what is the symbolic flood that is pursuing the woman? It is the antichrist's forces, and the earth opens up supernaturally and swallows them. The same was true of Pharaoh's army in that in pursuing Israel they were also swallowed up in the sea and destroyed.

It is also interesting to note that when the children of Israel got to the wilderness God fed them supernaturally with manna and the woman mentioned in Revelation 12 is to be fed by God as well.

I mentioned earlier that the antichrist confirms a covenant with Israel. Since he is only in power for seven years, and since the great tribulation period is only seven years long, then it must be concluded that the antichrist confirms a covenant with Israel when he first comes on the world scene.

The fact that the scripture makes this covenant a leading declaration it can mean only one thing – the Moslems want it as much as Israel. Why would the Moslems want it? I believe it is because Israel has soundly defeated them in another all-out war. The covenant period is confirmed to be for seven years.

Some talk about the covenant of peace being broken after three and a half years but that isn't entirely true. What infuriates the antichrist is the offering of sacrifices at the temple, and he does put a stop to them and it compels the religious Jews to flee into the wilderness. But most of Israel is secular as are the Jews in the United States, and they don't want to have anything to do with Judaism.

In Daniel 11.30 we find the antichrist shows regard to those who forsake the holy covenant. So, Israel, as a nation, is still at peace with their neighboring nations until nearing the end of the seven-year period when the battle of Armageddon forces them to engage in war again.

At the middle of the seven years of the tribulation the severity of events greatly increases as though they weren't bad enough already. This last period is known as the "Day of the Lord." In Malachi 4.5 the prophet describes the Day of the Lord by saying, "Behold I will send you Elijah the prophet before the coming of the great and dreadful day of the Lord." So, it is described as a time that people will dread and not a time that people will look forward to.

The apostle Paul explains the "Day of the Lord" very well in 1 Thessalonians 5.2-3,9. He said, "For you yourselves know perfectly that the day of the Lord so comes as a thief in the night. For when they say, 'peace and safety!' then sudden destruction comes upon them as labor pains upon a pregnant woman. And they shall not escape. [v.9] For God did not appoint us to wrath, but to obtain salvation through our Lord Jesus Christ." A couple of things stand out here. One, it is a time that brings sudden destruction from which people cannot escape and it also includes great calamity from God's wrath.

Paul makes another good point from verses four and five. He said, "But you brethren are not in darkness, so that this day should overtake you as a thief. You are all sons of light and sons of the day. We are not of the night nor of darkness."

When Paul says that we are sons of the day, he means sons of the Day of Grace. Therefore, he contrasts the Day of Grace to the day of darkness where grace is not found.

The apostle Paul made a second attempt to clarify the sequence of events to the Thessalonians in 2 Thessalonians 2.1-3. He said, "Now brethren, concerning the coming of our Lord Jesus Christ and our gathering together to Him, we ask you not to be soon shaken in mind or troubled, either by spirit or by word or by letter, as if from us, as though the day of the Lord has come. Let no one deceive you by any means; for that day will not come unless the falling away comes first and the man of sin is revealed, the son of perdition."

In verse two, some translations read "day of Christ" instead of day of the Lord (and they aren't the same), and it has caused confusion in the way the verse is interpreted. We know the correct word is "Lord" by the reaction of the Thessalonians when Paul said to them not to be alarmed or shaken in mind or troubled.

There were some in that community that were saying that the day of the Lord had come which then left them to believe they had missed the coming of Christ for His saints. But Paul wanted to reassure them that the day of the Lord had not come. Then he listed the events that had to take place before even the day of the Lord would come, namely a falling away, and the man of sin had to be revealed, none of which had occurred.

One needs to be aware that the apostasia, or the falling away, has now been fulfilled in our time. It isn't something we are still waiting for. The apostasia had not happened yet at the time of the Thessalonians in Paul's day. That fact alone puts us another big step closer to the time of the rapture.

So, what do we know about the falling away? In Asia minor the churches have dwindled to where they were taken over by the Muslims and many of the churches were made into Mosques. The Church attendance in Europe has fallen off dramatically to where very few attend anymore. In America church kids went off to college and were brainwashed into existentialism and so doubted their Biblical upbringing and their need to attend church anymore. Now we have a society with a very liberal viewpoint, so much so, that when they have to make a decision to choose between Biblical principles verses society's mores, they choose society's philosophy because political correctness has become the absolute standard to live by rather than the Word of God.

More of our Bible colleges have completely closed. Even the Pentagon is trying to force our chaplains out of the military if they oppose homosexuals and gay marriage. They are forbidden to pray in the name of Jesus. As they can, the ten commandments are being removed from government property. Many public schools have banned the Bible and prayer in the school. I could go on but it should be evident that we have seen the fulfillment of apostasia – the falling away. Yes, the rapture will occur first before the antichrist is revealed!

CHAPTER SIX

END OF THE AGE – END OF THE WORLD

There is a difference between the global events for "end of the age" and that of "end of the world." One thousand years separate these times from each other. Jesus mentions the end of the age in Matthew.

In Matthew 13.38-42 Jesus is explaining the parable of the wheat and the tares. There are two harvests – that of the "first fruits" and the last harvest called the "ingathering" at the end of the year, and they are described in Exodus 23.16, but Jesus in the parable was focusing on the last harvest.

He said, "The field is the world, the good seeds are the sons of the kingdom, but the tares are the sons of the wicked one. The enemy who sowed them is the devil, the harvest is the end of the age, and the reapers are the angels. Therefore, as the tares are gathered and burned in the fire, so it will be at the end of <u>this</u> age. The Son of Man will send out His angels, and they will gather our of His kingdom all things that offend, and those who practice lawlessness and will cast them into the furnace of fire. There will wailing and gnashing of teeth.

So, what Jesus is saying here is that when He <u>begins</u> His earthly reign, He will first of all, purge it of the unjust – those who were an offense, a stumbling block to any and all who were trying to enter into the kingdom of God, as well as those who are lawless. This is also clearly emphasized from 2 Thessalonians 1.6-10.

The apostle Paul was letting the Christians know their suffering for Christ was not in vain. He said, "Since it is a righteous thing with God to repay with tribulation those who trouble you and to give you who are troubled rest, with us, when the Lord Jesus is revealed from heaven with His mighty angels, in flaming fire taking vengeance on those who do not know God, and on those who do not obey the Gospel of our Lord Jesus Christ. These shall be punished with <u>ever-lasting</u> destruction from the presence of the Lord and from the glory of His power, when He comes in that day to be glorified in His saints…"

This clearly reveals <u>when</u> the end of the age is. What we see happening in the parable of the wheat and the tares is a <u>separating</u> of the just from the unjust. This is also known as the judgment of the nations. This is referenced in Matthew 25.31-32. Jesus said, "When the Son of Man comes in His glory, and all the holy angels with Him, He will sit on the throne of His glory. And **all nations** will be gathered before Him, and He will separate them one from another as a shepherd divides his sheep from the goats."

The picture that one needs to see here is that when a nation of people is brought before the Lord the angels separate out of that nation the just from the unjust. The just will go to the Lord's right hand and the unjust to His left hand until all are separated.

The just will be allowed to continue to live in Christ's kingdom but the unjust – well Jesus says it best in verse 41. "Then He will say to those on the left hand, 'Depart from Me you cursed, into the everlasting fire prepared for the devil and his angels. This judgment precedes the Great White Throne judgment by a thousand years.

If you remember from Matthew 13, those who will be purged out of Christ's kingdom are those who offend. Those who offend are those who prevent others from entering the kingdom of God as well as themselves.

This is a serious charge, so would you agree that the following categories make the list of those who offend? 1) Those who teach that the Bible is not true; 2) Those who teach that you won't have to be accountable to God for your life; 3) Those who try to get you to deny Christ or be killed; 4) Those who just simply lawlessly kill Christians because they are Christians; 5)Those who forbid you to hear the Word of God; 6) Those who slander and defraud others; 7) Those who promote false religions and doctrines; 8) Those who would forbid you to pray in the name of Jesus; 9) Those who would forbid the spread of the Gospel through missionaries in their country; 10) Those who promote an anti-God curriculum in the public schools and universities; 11) Those who suppress the truth about God or the Bible where not doing so would confirm the truth. This list could be expanded but you get the point.

It is amazing to me, that during the great tribulation time people will be subjected to severe judgments, and after all that they still do not repent of the murders, sorceries, sexual immorality or their thefts (Revelation 9.21). These judgments were intended for the purpose of putting pressure on people so they would repent, and so God wouldn't have to send them to a devil's hell.

So this is what brings the end of the age to a close. The good news is that those who repent and turn from their sins now and commit to His Lordship will be caught up from this escaping the sentence of damnation.

Now we turn our attention to the subject of the "end of the world." Jesus actually addresses it twice in Matthew chapter 24. In verses 35-36 Jesus said, "Heaven and earth will pass away, but My words will by no means pass away. But of that day and hour no one knows, not even the angels of heaven, but My Father only."

It should be obvious from these verses that the 1,000-year reign of Christ will have concluded as well as the event of the Great White Throne judgment.

The first time Jesus spoke of "the end" it has fostered a great deal of misunderstanding. In verse 14 He said, "And this gospel of the kingdom will be preached in all the world as a witness to all the nations and then the end will come."

Jesus was answering the disciple's question from the way it was asked in verse three. In verse three they asked, "And what will be the sign of Your coming and of the end of the world." More recent translations use the word "age" in place of the word "world." I noticed the King James translation, the Geneva Bible translation, and the Tyndale translation all use the word "world" and I believe that is the correct rendering.

The misunderstanding surrounding this verse goes farther than this. As an example, many have mis-read verse 14 to say, and this gospel of the kingdom will be preached in all the world as a witness to all the nations and then the rapture will come. The word "rapture" or the word "translation" are nowhere found in this verse. So, we really don't have grounds to believe that Jesus was referring to the rapture here. Therefore, if we hold to the view that Jesus is really referring to the end of the world as He was asked, it therefore implies, then that even during His millennial reign the Gospel will still go forth to the nations.

It will probably come as a surprise to some to discover the prophet Isaiah reveals that the Gospel will go forth even during the millennial reign of Christ. Isaiah 2.2-3 says, "Now it shall come to pass in the latter days that the mountain of the LORD'S house shall be established on the top of the mountains, and shall be exalted above the hills; and all nations shall flow to it. Many people will come and say 'Come, and let us go up to the mountain of the Lord, to the house of God of Jacob; He will teach us His ways, and we shall walk in His paths. 'For out of Zion shall go forth the law, **and the word of**

the Lord from Jerusalem." From this verse we find it is Israel who will now pick up the baton, so to speak, and carry the responsibility of getting the Gospel to the ends of the earth. This is more clearly seen in Isaiah 49.3, 6.

It reads, "and He said to me, you are **My servant O Israel in whom I will be glorified.** [v,6] Indeed He says, 'It is too small a thing that you should be My servant to raise up the tribes of Jacob and to restore the preserved ones of Israel; **I will also give you as a light to the Gentiles,** that you should be My salvation **to the ends of the earth.**'"

This shows the world still needs the Gospel preached to them during the millennial reign of Christ. Isaiah further implies this in chapter 52 verses seven and ten. It reads, "How beautiful upon the mountains are the feet of him who brings good news, who proclaims peace, who brings glad tiding of good things, **who proclaim salvation**, who says to Zion, your God reigns! [v.10] The Lord has made bare His holy arm in the eyes of all the nations; and all the ends of the earth shall see the salvation of our God."

Satan and his demons will be confined to the bottomless pit for the millennial reign of Christ so Satan won't be able to hinder the spread of the Gospel then. People will also have extended life spans allowing more time for the Gospel message to get to them. Yes, Jesus has indicated that by the end of the thousand years the whole world will have been reached.

It should be pointed out that "the end" here is not to be confused with the resurrection at the last day (John 11.24). The resurrection at the last day is simply the time of the resurrection of the righteous (Luke 14.14) and it signaled the end point for the Church dispensation. Once this translation of saints occurs no one else will get to be in the Bride of Christ – that door will be closed. Yes, there will be those who will be saved during the great tribulation time but they are a distinct category of saints narrowly identified as those saints who come out of the great tribulation (Revelation 7.13-14).

We must not forget there was an **appointed time** for Christ's first coming, and He kept it, and there is an **appointed time** for His next coming for the Church <u>and He won't be late for it</u>! We know that His appointed time for the rapture will take place in this generation!

The fulfillment of Psalm 2.1-5 is quickly approaching. It reads, "Why do the nations rage, and the people plot a vain thing? The kings of the earth set themselves and the rulers take counsel together against the Lord and against His anointed saying, 'Let us break their bonds in pieces and cast away their cords from us.' He who sits in the heavens shall laugh; the Lord shall hold them in derision. Then He shall speak to them in <u>His wrath</u> and distress them in His deep displeasure."

This passage speaks to those who are enemies of God and of Jesus Christ. All those <u>who reject</u> the saving grace of Jesus are His enemies. To be a little more specific it would include the anti-God professors in our universities and those who support them; radical or fundamental Muslims; Satanists and all other religions that reject Christ as Savior and Lord. They think (in vain) that if they just get rid of all the Christians they won't have to be accountable to God. This is why ISIS has been so bold in the middle east to slaughter Christians. ISIS is beyond barbaric; they are demonic. They thought their hour to succeed has come. But Satan has played his hand a little too soon. That authority has not been given to him until the last half of the great tribulation time.

God has a payback time and it is called the time of His wrath (Psalm 2.5). I've been intrigued by just one little aspect of God's wrath as described in the 6th trumpet judgment in Revelation 9.15. There we read, "So, the four angels who had been prepared for the hour and day and month and year were released to kill a third of mankind."

One might think this verse is just simply implying that the final moment arrived where the four angels could now unleash this judgment. The words "they were released" imply that, but it doesn't explain the words "for the hour and day and month and year." Those words reveal that is how long the four angels <u>had prepared</u> for this judgment to last. This reveals the sixth trumpet judgment, all by itself, will last a little over thirteen months and it will kill one third of mankind in that time period.

The destroying army involved numbers 200 million (v.16), and the judgment includes destroying winds (Rev.7.1) which will likely be caused from nuclear explosions. Only one nation on earth has the funds and manpower to field an army of 200 million and that is Red China. This has never been possible in any prior generation. What do you do with tens of millions of young men that will never have a wife because of China's former one child policy? You march them off to war to conquer nations. Since Communism doesn't believe in any God, China will come to believe they must stop this world's mad man (the antichrist), a Muslim who now wants to be worshipped as God, and annihilate his followers. Do you realize how many people one third of the earth's population is? That is over 2.3 billion people who are killed under this **one** judgment alone!

The sixth trumpet judgment is initiated in the latter part of <u>the first half</u> of the great tribulation period. We know this because the two witnesses are still on the earth during the sixth trumpet judgment, and their ministry was only to last for 3 ½ years. It is only <u>after</u> they are killed and resurrected that the 7th trumpet is sounded for more judgment.

Up until this point, the role of the 200-million-man army has not been directed at the antichrist but just to conquer as many nations as possible in its quest to be world conqueror. But China halts their war of aggression after 13 months perhaps to allow for burying the dead and for resupplying their forces and take the time needed to re-evaluate their next course of action. One thing we are not told is how many of their own forces were killed during this time. Later, we know from Revelation 16.12-14, that this formidable army moves again from the east with the intent to destroy the antichrist's army and this culminates in the battle of Armageddon (Revelation 16.16).

I believe this is the time Jesus spoke of when He said, "And unless these days were shortened no flesh would be saved" (Matthew 24.21-22).

CHAPTER SEVEN

What Do You Do With Truth?

There have been some flagrant accusations made against Christianity that merit a response. These accusations are not new. Their purpose has been to keep people from knowing the truth. You may recognize some of these accusations: 1) the Bible has been corrupted and can't be relied upon; 2) Jesus never said the things the Bible says He said; 3) Jesus didn't die on the cross; 4) Jesus never rose from the dead; 5) Jesus didn't ascend into heaven.

Satan is wanting to annul these major tenets of Christianity through these accusations. So, let's examine the first accusation that the Bible has been corrupted. To start with, the accuser has a real problem because he would only know it has been corrupted if he had an uncorrupted version to compare it to. The best argument the accuser has is merely an assumption for which he has no proof!

Let's look at the Bible's declaration concerning itself. In Psalm 138.2 it says, "...For You have magnified Your word <u>above </u>all Your name." This implies the highest honor that can be given is given to the word of God! The prophet Isaiah said, "...the word of our God stands forever" (Isaiah 40.8). So, here we have the Bible's declaration that it is the truth. A Bible scholar would respond by pointing out some things.

First, the Bible was written over some 1500 years so most of the writers did not know each other personally and therefore they could not collude with each other what they were going to write. For example, king David lived a few centuries after Moses so he couldn't change Mose's historical account (had he even wanted to) without introducing a conflict of interest in the Pentateuch. This never happened.

Secondly, some of the earliest version of the Bible were the Syriac Bible available in the first and second century, the Vulgate by 400 A.D., the Masoretic text by 500 A.D., and they could compare the Old Testament with the Septuagint written about 250 B.C. The Septuagint Bible was the Bible used by Jesus and the apostles because it so accurately pointed to Jesus as the Messiah. But in the second century A.D., a revision of the Septuagint was made to change the wording so it wouldn't portray Christ as the Messiah. So, then the Christians began using the Hebrew writings. The revisionists were not completely successful because they overlooked Isaiah chapter 53 which gave very specific information about the vicarious suffering of the Messiah.

It is true that scholars wondered for centuries how accurate the Bible we had was. Then a remarkable thing happened in the 20th century with the discovery of the Dead Sea Scrolls. They predated our oldest versions by about 1,000 years. When they compared the Dead Sea Scrolls with versions, we already had, it was discovered there was very little difference between them – only a few very minor scribal errors which did not compromise any Biblical doctrine. So, the Holy Bible has been preserved with great accuracy. Those who want to continue the reliability debate only do so because they do not want to believe the facts as the really are.

The Bible is further confirmed through archaeological discoveries of the cities and towns mentioned in scripture as well as kings who ruled over nations and empires during Biblical times. In fact, the documentation for this has been so extensive that it has posed real problems for the skeptics.

Consider the next accusation that Jesus never said the things the Bible says He said. First of all, you can't deny or change what was said because it has been documented for all to read. Secondly, these statements the Bible said He spoke were all said by the same central figure. Thirdly, no one else takes credit for the things Jesus said but Jesus, and all the eye witnesses of that time credit Jesus for making His statements. It was His teachings and His commandments and His miracles that formed a large following of disciples. His disciples would not have been willing to follow Him **or give up their very lives for Him if He had been a fraud.** Jesus, Himself, did not deny the things concerning His Deity and it got Him crucified. Jesus was not likely taking the rap for someone else and someone else is never named. When His disciples evangelized, they never proclaimed the words of someone else – only the message of Jesus as Savior of the world. I would say the burden of proof rests on the accuser as to who said the words the Bible attributes to Jesus.

Let's consider the next accusation that Jesus never died on the cross. The main question I have for the accuser is, can you point to even one case where a person was crucified <u>as Jesus was</u>, having first been beaten with whips that ripped His back into shreds causing a massive amount of blood loss, and then have large spikes driven into His hands and feet causing even more blood loss, and then have a soldier pierce His side with a spear draining the blood from His heart, who could then be able to come down from the cross after many hours later without having died?

Secondly, Pilot did not allow Jesus to be taken down from the cross without ascertaining from the Centurion that Jesus was indeed dead. Again the burden of proof that Jesus didn't die rests with the accuser. Denying reality does not change historical fact!

Then there are the accusations that Jesus didn't rise from the dead or ascend into heaven. Both are included together here because both events had many eye witnesses. The first evidence that Jesus rose from the dead was the soldiers who were assigned to guard the tomb fled into the city to tell the chief priests what happened. So, we need to ask why were they so fearful and emotional if nothing had happened? They were fearful because they saw the power of God in action in Jesus' resurrection and those soldiers were not about to challenge Him! **They fled!**

When the disciples were later in Jerusalem proclaiming that Jesus was alive and that it was He who healed the lame man it upset the chief priests who wanted to shut them up. The only way they could possibly do that would be to produce the dead body of Jesus but they couldn't because He had risen from the dead and they knew that!

Then there was the occasion when Jesus appeared to His disciples in the upper room when the doors were locked. They believed, after He showed them His hands and feet where they had been pierced by the nails that fastened Him to the cross.

The apostle Paul said that more than 500 saw Him at one time (1 Corinthians 15.6). At Bethany while Jesus was among His disciples He ascended right before their eyes into a cloud and into heaven (Luke 24.50-51).

There is more evidence to believe that Jesus is the real deal. The Old Testament proclaimed Jesus would come as a suffering Messiah and also later as a kingly Messiah. Well, Jesus and only Jesus has fulfilled all those prophecies of Him coming as a suffering Messiah! Let's look next at some of those prophecies.

The prophet Daniel revealed the Messiah would be cut off but not for Himself (Daniel 9.26). The prophet David revealed He would be given gall and vinegar to drink (Psalm 69,21), that they would pierce His hands and His feet (Psalm 22.16) and that they would divide His garments and cast lots for His clothing (Psalm 22.18). The prophet Isaiah revealed He would be beaten (Isaiah 50.6 and 53.5) and that He would bear the iniquity of our sins (Isaiah 53.6). The prophet Zechariah revealed He would be betrayed for 30 pieces of silver (Zechariah 11.12). His resurrection was foretold in Psalm 16.10.

These prophecies in Isaiah were given about 790 years before they were fulfilled; those in Daniel 640 years before, and those in Zechariah 550 years before being fulfilled. But here's the thing – they were all fulfilled <u>in the time</u> of Jesus' ministry <u>by Jesus</u>! **No one else has been able to make that claim**, and that is very significant! Furthermore, there are no other books that have prophesied the birth, the time and place of birth, the life and death and resurrection of an individual centuries before those events were to be fulfilled of someone other than Christ! Are you starting to see the significance of the One called Jesus yet?

One of the things that amazes me is how God works behind the scenes to bring about the fulfillment of His word. Consider that the prophet Micah foretold, 750 years before the birth of Christ, that He would be born in Bethlehem. That wouldn't necessarily be a big deal if Joseph and Mary were already living in Bethlehem, but they were not. They were living in Nazareth of Galilee and showed no interest in going to Bethlehem. But God moved on a Roman king to issue a decree for everyone to go register at their home of birth. This forced Joseph and Mary to make the trip from Nazareth to Bethlehem. If they had been even one day late Jesus would have been born somewhere else but they made it just in time. If the Roman decree had been issued too late Jesus would not have been born there either. The time and location of His birth was fulfilled with precision. This again shows how reliable Bible prophecy is!

So, who is this God who works behind the scenes to fulfill His great plan? Well, Abraham knew Him, so, let's see how Abraham addressed God, and how God addressed Himself to Abraham. In Genesis 14.22 Abraham said to the king of Sodom, "…I have raised my hand to the Lord (Yehovah), God (Almighty), the Possessor of heaven and earth." So, he addresses God as Yehovah and the Almighty.

When God addresses <u>Himself to Abraham</u> (in Genesis 15.7) He said to him, "I am the Lord (Yehovah), who brought you out of Ur of the Chaldeans, to give you this land to inherit it." Then again, in Genesis 17.1 God addresses Abraham this way, "…I am Almighty God (Almighty); walk before Me and be blameless."

Last of all, in Genesis 17.3 it says, "Then Abram fell on his face, and God (Elohiym) talked with him…" So, in this verse, God is also known to Abraham as Elohiym. Continuing in verses 7-8 God says, "And I will establish My covenant between Me and you and your descendants after you in their generations for an everlasting covenant to be God (Elohiym) to you and your descendants after you. Also, I will give you and your descendants after you the land in which you are a stranger all the land of Canaan as an everlasting possession: and I will be their God" (Elohiym).

Abraham's descendants were to address God as Elohiym and Yehovah. So, the descendants of Abraham who recognize, and address God by these names reveal who the true heirs to the land are. Abraham never addressed God as Allah nor did God address Himself to Abraham as Allah. Therefore, Allah and Jehovah <u>are not</u> the same God.

Now that we have looked at how precise some of these prophecies have been about Jesus, we should also consider some of Jesus' own prophecies and how they are impacting this 1948 generation.

In Luke's gospel, chapter 21, Jesus prophesied that **"nation will arise against nation."** So far, in **this** generation over 70 wars occurred <u>just from 1948</u> and, of course, that would not count WWI or WWII.

In the same chapter Jesus prophesied that **"kingdom would rise against kingdom."** So far, there have been over 145 conflicts <u>just since 1948</u>. Kingdom conflicts being defined where a new foundation of power is trying to be established through conflict.

Jesus also prophesied that there would be **great earthquakes** in various places. I define a great earthquake where there is a significant loss of human life. So far, there have been over 74 such earthquakes from 1948 that have taken over 1,558,390 lives.

Jesus also prophesied that there would be **famines**. Since 1948 over 23,600,000 have died from famine.

Jesus prophesied **many would be hated and killed for His name's sake.** Since 1948 we are told over 6.93 million have been martyred for Christ around the world.

Jesus prophesied that there would be **pestilences.** Since 1948 over 31 million have died from various pestilences. Twenty-five million just from aids alone. As recently as 1967 two million died from small pox.

So how big do the numbers have to be before you say these prophecies of Jesus have certainly been fulfilled in this generation? The point is, what Jesus said would happen in this generation has happened!

So now what do we do with knowing that Bible prophecy is 100% accurate? Since so much of it centers around God's great unfolding plan and the center of His plan centers around His Son Jesus then we need to understand what this all means.

A brief summary of what lies ahead is found in Philippians 2.9-11. Speaking of Jesus; "...God also has highly exalted Him and given Him the name which is above every name, that at the name of Jesus every knee should bow of those in heaven, and those on earth, and of those under the earth, and that every tongue should confess that Jesus Christ is Lord to the glory of God the Father." Can you think of anyone who these verses will offend? How about Satan for starters, and every other religious leader in the world who isn't a Christian, and those who presently reject Christianity period. This is one reason why so many nations are out to destroy Israel because their existence is a testimony to the fulfillment of Bible prophecy and unless they can change that they will have to admit the Bible is true; its prophecies being true, and that is the last thing they want to accept.

Is there anything more sad than those who are deceived and who are being deceived? For example, lifted up on the same pedestal are those who place Judaism, Christianity and Islam. There are supposed to be enough similarities between them that they should be able to live together in peace. Judaism and Islam are similar in that they both reject Christ as the Way and they both reject Christ's Deity. His Deity was proclaimed clearly by the prophet Isaiah. In Isaiah 7.14 it says, "Therefore the Lord Himself will give you a sign, 'Behold the virgin shall conceive and bear a Son and shall call His name Immanuel.'"

The name **Immanuel means God with us.** In Isaiah 9.6 it says, "For unto us a child is born, unto us a Son is given; and the government will be upon His shoulder. And His name will be called Wonderful, Counselor, **Mighty God**..." These prophecies concerning the Messiah Jesus were documented approximately 750 years before He came.

So, how would His Deity be recognized if He truly was God in man? Expressing His Deity would be to do supernaturally what no other man could do. For example, He turned water into wine (John 2.2-11).

He cleansed lepers (Luke 7.11-15); fed 5,000 people with only five loaves and two fish (Luke 9.13-17); gave sight to two blind men (Matthew 9.27-31); walked on the water of the sea of Galilee (Matthew 14.24-33) and there are many more miracles recorded which can be cited, but surely one can see these miracles confirmed His Deity. The common people in His day were in awe that He could do these mighty miracles (Mark 6.2).

Those who reject Christ have a real problem and may not even realize they have a problem. Their problem is defying truth. Truth is expressed in <u>fulfilled Bible prophecy</u> concerning Christ! Yes, many will continue to reject Christ not understanding the peril that awaits them in doing so. There are really two camps here.

The first are those who have convinced themselves that it doesn't matter what you believe. The second are those who hold to a religion that believes they are right and Christianity is wrong. So, what's the problem? The problem is, both groups are even now facing the <u>fact that all</u> Bible prophecy concerning Christ is being fulfilled without any error! What do you do with 100% accuracy? Ignore it Disbelieve it? Or believe it?

Jesus commented on a question that was posed to Him. "Then one said to Him, Lord are there few who are saved? 'And He said to them, strive to enter through the narrow gate, for many I say to you, will seek to enter and will not be able'" (Luke 13.23-24). In Matthew 7.13-14 Jesus said, "Enter by the narrow gate; for wide is the gate and broad is the way that leads to destruction, and there are many who go in by it. Because narrow is the gate and difficult is the way which leads to life, and there are few who find it."

Truth is actually alive in the person of Jesus Christ! The miracles that were performed at the hands of the apostles would not have happened if Jesus hadn't rose from the dead. Saul, the Christian hater, would not have been converted to Christianity if he hadn't had a personal encounter with Jesus Christ. The book of the Revelation of Jesus Christ would not have been written if Jesus hadn't rose from the dead. In Revelation 1.18 Jesus says, "I am He who lives, and was dead, and behold, I am alive forevermore."

The coming big surprise is stated in Revelation 1.7. It says, "Behold, He is coming with clouds, and every eye will see Him, even they who pierced Him. And all the tribes of the earth will mourn because of Him. Even so, Amen."

CHAPTER EIGHT

Resurrection of Life and Restoration

To understand how prophetic events will unfold one must consider God's thinking that goes into His great plan. For example, in John chapter five, Jesus was attempting to get His hearers to understand that **He is** the resurrection and the life, and then went on to say there would be two resurrections. Verse 28 and 29 read, "…the hour is coming in which all who are in the graves will hear His voice and come forth – those who have done good, to the resurrection of life, and those who have done evil, to the resurrection of condemnation."

So, Jesus explains that there are two types of resurrections. One is to life, and one is to condemnation. It is Revelation chapter 20 that reveals the resurrection to condemnation doesn't occur until a thousand years after the resurrection to life has been completed.

In addition, we discover something else when we read verses 4-5. It says, "…Then I saw the souls of those who had been beheaded for their witness to Jesus and for the word of God, who had not worshipped the beast, or his image, and had not received his mark on their foreheads or on their hands. And they lived and reigned with Christ for a thousand years. But the rest of the dead did not live again <u>until the thousand years were finished</u>. This is the first resurrection."

The only saints described in these verses are the great tribulation saints and yet they are declared to be in the first resurrection. Why is that? Because it is a resurrection unto life. It is verse six that reveals the first resurrection consists of parts. It reads, "Blessed and holy is he who has <u>part</u> in the first resurrection..."

When Jesus was resurrected it was to life; when the two witnesses are raised after three days it will be to life, and when the rapture occurs it will be a resurrection to life. God considers all of these to be a part of the first resurrection – the resurrection to life.

Now to know precisely when the great tribulation saints are resurrected all we have to do is note where they follow in the sequence of events that is given to us. We observe this sequence beginning in chapter 19 and verse 14 where it shows the armies of heaven following Jesus to earth. It reads, "And the armies in heaven, clothed in fine linen, white and clean, followed Him on white horses." Verse 19 shows the impending battle will be waged against the earth's armies. It says, "And I saw the beast, the kings of the earth, and their armies, gathered together to make war against Him, who sat on the horse and against His army." Next the beast and false prophet are cast alive into the lake of fire (v.20) followed by Satan being bound and cast into the bottomless pit (chapter 20 verses 2-3) followed by thrones of judgment being set up (v.4) <u>and then</u> the great tribulation saints are resurrected.

There is a particular group of saints that will be resurrected to life that are Daniel's people, that is, the Old Testament saints. Notice how Daniel 12.1-2 reads, "At that time Michael shall stand up, the great prince who stands watch over the sons of <u>your people</u>; and there shall be a time of trouble, such as never was since there was a nation, even to that time. And <u>at that time</u> your people shall be delivered, everyone who is found written in the book. And many of those **who sleep in the dust of the earth shall awake**, some to everlasting life..."

The description of the time of trouble here is referring to what is known as the time of Jacob's trouble, and it commences half way through the seven-year tribulation period. Jesus established when this would be in Matthew 24.14 and 21, and is also confirmed in Daniel 9.27 to occur at this time. So we see the Old Testament saints are resurrected half way through the tribulation time.

I find it interesting that the Bride of Christ will be with Jesus before the Old Testament saints are resurrected. Is this related to Jesus' statement that the first shall be last and the last shall be first?

I also find an interesting link between the very first two prophecies of scripture and to note their relationship. In the first prophecy, God was speaking to Satan, in Genesis 3.15 and said, "And I will put enmity between you and the woman, and between your seed and her seed; He shall bruise your head..." So in this first prophecy we see that the significant person here is Christ who will subdue Satan at some point in time.

The second prophecy, in scripture, was given by Enoch. Now Enoch, himself is a type of the Bride of Christ. There are 365 days in a Gentile year and Enoch lived 365 years and then was raptured. He was raptured because he had a relationship with God, for the scripture says that he walked with God. Jesus' bride will have a relationship with Him and be fully dedicated to Him. It is interesting that Enoch's name means dedication. Enoch was the seventh from <u>Adam</u>, Colossians 2.10 says, "and you are <u>complete in Him</u> who is the Head of all principality and power."

Enoch's prophecy is not found in the Old Testament but in the book of Jude verses 14-15. It reads, "Now Enoch, the seventh from Adam prophesied about these men also saying, 'Behold the Lord comes with ten thousands of His saints to execute judgment on all to convict who are ungodly among them of all their ungodly deeds which they have committed in an ungodly way...'"

So, this second prophecy portrays the Bride of Christ as being with Jesus once you understand the prophecy. This reveals how much Jesus values His relationship with His bride in that the second prophecy includes <u>the presence of His bride</u>.

I'm sure you get the part that parallels the Revelation passage of the saints coming back with Jesus to wage war on the ungodly. But how many stop to think about how those saints got to be with Jesus in the first place before they came back with Him?

Those saints that are coming back with Him (Rev.19) to conquer the ungodly enemies of Christ can't be great tribulation saints since those saints will not have been resurrected yet. Therefore, those saints who accompany Jesus at His return must be pre-tribulation saints, those who have been recipients of a pretrib rapture.

Verse 14 of Jude doesn't say Jesus is coming back with ten thousand saints but rather with ten thousands (in the plural) of them. That means multiplied ten thousands. Just ten thousand times ten thousand is 100 million. The earth will then be faced with an impossibly huge heavenly army and the following words of Jesus will be fulfilled at that time. He said, "Then the sign of the Son of Man will appear in heaven, and then all the tribes of the earth will mourn, and they will see the Son of Man coming on the clouds of heaven with power and great glory" (Matthew 24.30).

I believe Jesus is in love with His bride. When Jesus spoke of Father God, He would call Him Theos, but when He spoke of Himself, He used the word Kurios. Now when Jesus quotes the greatest commandment in Matthew 22.37, He said, "You shall love the Lord (Kurios) your God with all your heart, with all your soul, and with all your mind." So, Jesus was referring to Himself when He was quoting this scripture and it showed relationship with Him was at the top of His list of what was important!

This chapter will be closed out by viewing the apostle Peter's understanding of prophetic scripture. Peter was addressing a crowd that was marveling at the healing of the lame man, but Peter was attempting to focus the crowd's attention on Jesus. In Acts 3.18-21, 24, he said, "But those things which God foretold by the mouth of all His prophets that the Christ would suffer, He has thus fulfilled. Repent therefore, and be converted that your sins may be blotted out, so that times of refreshing may come from the presence of the Lord, and that He may send Jesus Christ, who was preached to you before whom heaven must receive until the times of restoration of all things, which God has spoken by the mouth of all His holy prophets since the world began. [v.24] Yes, and all the prophets from Samuel and those who follow, as many as have spoken, have also foretold these days."

When Peter mentioned Samuel it really piqued my interest. I wanted to know what Samuel had to say about Jesus so I went back and reread first and second Samuel. I read through the first book of Samuel and there was nothing said about Him, and there was nothing in the second book of Samuel until I got to the deliverance chapter toward the end of the book. Many would probably miss the prophetic significance of this chapter, but the true believer could grasp it. Why? Because Jesus said to His disciples, "…it has been given to you to know the mysteries of the kingdom of heaven…" Matthew 13.11.

The prophet David is speaking in second Samuel chapter 22, and identifies who he is talking about in verses 2-4. He said, "The Lord is my Rock and my fortress and my Deliverer. The God of my strength in whom I will trust; my shield and the horn of my salvation, my stronghold and my refuge; my Savior. You save me from violence. I will call upon the Lord who is worthy to be praised; so shall I be saved from my enemies."

We would recognize that our Rock and our Savior is Jesus. Those words, "…You save me from violence" is something our generation can identify with. Jesus said, "as it was in the days of Noah so also will the coming of the Son of Man be." In Genesis 6.11 it said the following about Noah's time. "The earth also was corrupt before God and the earth was filled with violence."

Going back to 2 Samuel 22.17 it speaks prophetically about the mystery of deliverance. "He sent <u>from above. He took me. He drew me out</u> of many waters. [v.18] He delivered me…" Does the rapture need to be portrayed with an analogy any better than this? I don't think so. Being drawn "out of many waters" is symbolism for being taken out from many peoples. Now in verse 20 notice where to. "He brought me out into a broad place; He delivered me because He delighted in me." So why be taken to a broad place? (In the Hebrew, it also tends to mean a good place).

Well, notice what it says about those who are raptured in Revelation 5.9. "…You are worthy to take the scroll and open its seals; for You were slain and have redeemed us to God by Your blood out of every tribe and tongue and people and nation." Then in verse 11 it says, "Then I looked and I heard the voice of many angels around the throne, the living creatures, and the elders; and the number of them was ten thousand times ten thousand and thousands of thousands." So, you see a broad expansive place is needed to accommodate so many in one place.

Notice what Jesus says, in Revelation 22.17, at the time of His coming. "And behold I am coming quickly and My reward is with Me <u>to give</u> to everyone according to his work." Now notice what it says in verse 21 in 2 Samuel 22. <u>"The Lord rewarded me</u> according to my righteousness according to the cleanness of my hands He has recompensed me."

So, Peter was correct when he deduced that in the book of Samuel it spoke of Jesus, and in Acts 3.21 that Jesus would bring about the restoration of all things. What has to be restored is bringing us back from a fallen state to a state where we will <u>abide in His will</u> once again. In John 17.23 Jesus prayed for this to happen. And John said, "…we know that when He is revealed we shall be like Him, for we shall see Him as He is" 1 John 3.2.

So, Peter wanted his audience to know that Jesus wasn't someone you could dismiss as being out of sight – out of mind. His healing the lame man was evidence Jesus was very much alive.

CHAPTER NINE

THE TEN HORNS AND THE LAST TRUMPET

Until recently, prophecy scholars have missed an important part of the prophetic picture. First let me state what prophecy students have got right. The fourth beast of Daniel 7.7, 23 represented the region of the old Roman empire. In the end-time ten horns were to emerge from this same region. But the next part, prophecy students got wrong in believing that the ten horns represented ten nations from the region of the old Roman empire. Daniel 7.24 tells us we should be looking for 10 kings that shall arise, not 10 nations. The verse reads, "The ten horns are ten kings who shall arise from this kingdom…"

Some might argue that some of those European nations already have kings, which is true, and I would add that since they are already kings over their respective countries, they then already have their own kingdoms. So why is this a problem? Revelation 17.12 says the following: "The ten horns which you saw are ten kings <u>who have received **no** kingdom as yet </u>but they receive authority for one hour as kings with the beast.

So, what we should expect to see are ten men who have great power probably in the form of great wealth that are pushing for a one world government, and that will arise from the region of the old Roman empire. In the book of James chapter five verses 1-8 it indicates they are rich and in verse three it says, "You have heaped up treasure in the last days." The time component here places them in our generation – "last days." The word "heaped," in the Greek, means amassed. The first part of verse three indicates the type of wealth they amassed is gold and silver. Every once in a while, you will hear of a depository with a basement containing literally tons of gold bars. Might there be a connection here?

The scripture says they acquired their wealth through fraudulent means (v.4) even to the point of having people killed (v.6). James describes them as having hearts and minds that are evil, as does the Septuagint Bible in Daniel 7.24. The verse reads, "As for its ten horns ten kings shall arise and another shall arise behind them who shall surpass in evil all the previous ones." Yes, they are evil and the antichrist will be even more evil than they.

So, when is all this supposed to be fulfilled? Well, again in James 5.3 it said in the "last days" and in verse eight when "the coming of the Lord is at hand." In other words, the generation we are living in. Daniel 7.24 also says, "The ten are ten horns who shall <u>arise</u> from this kingdom. That word "arise" means to appoint, to set up; make to stand. So, who does the selecting and appointing of these ten? Will it be through the Bilderbergers, the European Union, the UN? The point is, there will be ten who will rule over ten regions in the progression toward world government. According to the prophecy, this step is accomplished **before** the antichrist emerges to his prominent position.

Next, you need to see even though these ten have great power, <u>authority has to be given to them</u> before they can rule (Rev.17.12). Who gives them this authority? After they have this authority they turn and give the antichrist their full support. Revelation 17.13 says, "These are of one mind and they will give their power <u>and</u> authority to the beast." Did you notice, from this verse, that they weren't given power. They already had that. All they needed was authority to act.

<u>From Revelation chapter 17</u>, we know they will aid in bringing about the final collapse of the United States so they

can rule over the ten regions of the earth. We need to keep watch of anything that will bring about the establishment of these ten. What will cause their emergence? I believe it will be distress of nations that Jesus spoke of. That is usually the result of failing economies, inflated currencies and the pressure of expanding conflicts coupled now with the large movement of immigrants.

THE LAST TRUMPET

In the past there has been some controversy over when the sounding of the last trumpet takes place. The sounding of the last trumpet being supposedly in reference to when the saints are caught up. A person once said, "Well it's a no brainer. During the time of the seven trumpet judgments when the seventh one sounds that is the last one." Actually, it isn't the last one as we will see in a moment.

First of all, we should not confuse the time of judgments and the time of deliverance. The seventh trumpet deals with judgment not with the deliverance of the saints.

We need to look at the statement the apostle Paul made in 1 Corinthians 15.51-52. "Behold I tell you a mystery: We shall not all sleep, but we shall all be changed – in a moment, in the twinkling of an eye, at the last trumpet. For the trumpet will sound and the dead will be raised incorruptible, and we shall be changed."

The previous verse 50 establishes who Paul is talking about and that is all those who will inherit the kingdom of God right down to the last of them. We can understand this a little bit better by asking a question. Will Daniel's people, the Jews, who have their names written in the Book of Life inherit the kingdom of God? The answer is yes. Will the Bride of Christ the Church, inherit the kingdom of God? Again, the answer is yes. Will the great tribulation saints inherit the kingdom of God? The answer is yes as they are the final ingathering of the Feast of Harvest, the good harvest, and these in particular, are the ones who hear the "last trumpet call."

Jesus pointed out that this is when the last call is sounded (in Matthew 24.29-31) and it is understood by the context that it isn't happening in the middle of the tribulation but at the end of it.

Let's read those three verses. "Immediately after the tribulation of those days the sun will be darkened, and the moon will not give its light; the stars will fall from heaven, and the powers of the heavens will be shaken. Then the sign of the Son of Man will appear in heaven, and then all the tribes of the earth will mourn and they will see the Son of Man coming on the clouds of heaven with power and great glory. And He will send His angels **with a great sound of a trumpet**, and they will gather together His elect from the four winds, from one end of heaven to the other."

There is something else to be picked up on from the Corinthian chapter 15 passage. The main theme Paul was addressing was that of being "changed" from mortality to immortality at the last trump. So, what Paul was saying there was that those (the last to inherit the kingdom) will be the last ones to be changed and receive immortality.

In a different letter the apostle Paul does address a pretrib rapture in 1 Thessalonians 4.16-17. "For the Lord Himself will descend from heaven with a shout, with the voice of an archangel, and with the trumpet of God, and the dead in Christ will rise first. Then we who are alive and remain shall be caught up together with them in the clouds to meet the Lord in the air. And thus, we shall always be with the Lord."

You observed the word "trumpet" used here with the catching away of the saints but what was missing? It was the word "last" because this pretrib rapture trumpet call is not the last one. The last one comes at the end of the tribulation not prior to it.

CHAPTER TEN

Revealing Two Mysteries

For years I wondered about the meaning of the scripture found in Joel 2.30, but now I believe it has given up its secret. It reads, "And I will show wonders in the heavens and in the earth; blood and fire and pillars of smoke."

The "show" in the Hebrew is "nathan" and can have a wide variety of meanings. This word can mean "cause," "grant" and also "bring forth."

This brings us to the next word which is "wonders." It also can have other meanings and the one most often read is "signs." The Septuagint Bible probably renders it best when it uses the word "portent." In other words, what will be seen and experienced may be bad but after this even worse things will happen.

Now when I first read Joel 2.30, I thought this must be speaking about volcanic eruptions where you have belching lava and plumes of smoke and I suppose one could hold to that view but I'm inclined to believe it is speaking about something else. There are volcanoes erupting around the world all the time but they really don't account for the word "blood" because most of the time people have enough time to get away from an eruption.

In the context of this verse, the word "blood" is significant because it represents loss of life. There is something that fits this criterion and it is exploding nuclear warheads from missiles.

If we use acceptable alternate Hebrew meanings in verse 30 it might read; And I will grant (or allow) portents in the heavens and in the earth; blood and fire and pillars of smoke.

This is definitely an event that would cause a large loss of life. The fireball from a nuclear explosion would incinerate everything in a one mile radius and start fires out to a 15-mile radius from just a small four megaton bomb. Immediately afterward you have a towering pillar of smoke that forms a mushroom cloud.

If you noticed from this verse, it is not depicting a solitary event because the word "pillars" is in the plural. This indicates this is a sequel of events that are occurring. Also, according to the sequence of events given in Joel chapter two, it shows this will occur <u>before</u> the "awesome day of the Lord" which will be even worse than the foregoing nuclear exchange.

The Lord is giving us important information as to how awful or terrible the "day of the Lord" will be. We know these words in Joel were written for our generation because only our generation has knowledge of what devastation can be brought about by a nuclear missile, so we know we are living in the generation in which this will occur.

Verse 31 tells us what happens after these missiles come down out of the heavens or the sky to do their destructive work. The verse reads, "The sun shall be turned into darkness and the moon into blood..." Scientists have said that a large nuclear exchange could cause a nuclear winter from the radiated debris that would go up into the atmosphere and the darkened skies would make the moon look blood red.

There are a growing number of nations with this nuclear capability such as: Red China, Russia, North Korea, Pakistan, the UK, the US, India, France, and Israel. Iran is also striving to be in this elite group. These nations circle the earth with their nuclear capability and if they all got involved in a WWIII conflict this would produce a global phenomenon unlike anything this world has ever seen before.

Is it likely? Unfortunately, the answer is yes. Why? Because if one of those nuclear powers was left unharmed, they would then become the dominant world power and the other nuclear powers would not allow this. This is what I was told when going through my nuclear power training in the Navy.

It is just amazing that the Bible continues to inform us of future events, that will take place in our generation well before they happen. Can't say we haven't been informed.

Now let's look at the second mystery found in Isaiah chapter 17. Verse one says, "The burden against Damascus. Behold Damascus will cease from being a city and it will be a ruinous heap."

A few years after this prophecy it was conquered by the Assyrians in 732 B.C., but did that fulfill this prophecy? The answer is no. Because even after it was conquered it didn't cease from being a city. The fact that it is still a city lets us know this prophecy has an end-time fulfillment yet to be realized.

We are given some clues as to when this will happen. It will be at a time when the cities of Aroer are also forsaken (v.2). The cities of Aroer were located east of the Dead Sea in what we call Jordan today but was in the Syrian domain when this was prophesied. The next clue is in verse four. "In that day it shall come to pass that the glory of Jacob will wane, and the fatness of his flesh grow lean."

So, when does Israel's glory fade and grow dim? It is at the battle of Armageddon. Zechariah 13.8-9 makes it clear when this is. "And it shall come to pass in all the land, says the Lord, that two thirds in it shall be cut off and die, but one third shall be left in it: I will bring the one third through the fire, will refine them as silver is refined and test them as gold is tested. They will call on My name, and I will answer them. I will say this is My people; and each one will say, The Lord is my God."

This accords with the words in Isaiah 17.7. "In that day a man will look to his Maker, and his eyes <u>will have respect</u> for the Holy One of Israel." In all honesty, Israel is not going to respect Jesus until He comes back and fights for Israel! This clinches the time period for Damascus' demise!

Now there is more going on here in this passage of scripture. Isaiah 17.9 says, "In that day his strong cities will be as a forsaken bough and an uppermost branch, which they left <u>because of the children of Israel</u>; and there will be desolation." Why do these areas of Syria and Jordan become desolate at this time? It is to fulfill God's promise to Abraham (Genesis 15.18-21), Isaac (Genesis 26.4), and Jacob (Genesis 28.13-14) that these lands would become Israel's.

The last clue we will look at comes from Isaiah 17 verses 12 and 13. "Woe to the multitude of many people who make a noise like the roar of the seas, and to the rushing of nations that make a rushing like the rushing of mighty waters! The nations will rush like the rushing of many waters; but God will rebuke them and they will flee far away..." Now notice how this ties in with Revelation 19.15. "Now out of His mouth goes a sharp sword that with it He should strike the nations..." The person in this verse, is of course, referring to Jesus because in the next verse He is described as "King of Kings and Lord of Lords." At this point, in Revelation chapter 19 Jesus is returning with the armies of heaven to end the battle of Armageddon.

So, the fulfillment of this prophecy concerning Damascus is a few years off and we don't need to expect it to happen right away.

CHAPTER ELEVEN

America In Prophecy

Most prophetic teaching has not included references to America since it wasn't recognized in Scripture. It's true, the word America isn't in the Bible in the text as we read it (although, it is in the Bible codes). America's identity has been hidden through symbolism and analogy, similar to the way parables are veiled.

The word "Bible" is not in any of its books, yet we recognize those books as being the Bible. At one time, I thought anyone who believed America was Babylon of the end-time was way off in left field until I became open enough, after several years, to study it out for myself.

We begin in the book of Isaiah chapter 47 and verse one and we read, "Come down and sit in the dust O virgin daughter of Babylon; sit on the ground without a throne O daughter of the Chaldeans! For you shall no longer be called tender and delicate." This passage seems to speaking about Babylon and you might assume it to be referring to historical Babylon. But, if you read this chapter carefully you will find over a half dozen places that reveal why this can't be referring to the ancient kingdom of Babylon, and this is key to understanding the prophecy.

Reading again verse one it says, "Come down and sit in the dust, O virgin daughter of Babylon; sit on the ground without a throne, O daughter of the Chaldeans for you shall no longer be called tender and delicate." The first clue, that this isn't speaking about historical Babylon is it specifies "daughter of Babylon."

The next clue is borne out from the Hebrew with regard to the word "virgin." "Virgin" can also imply "separate." So, the phrase can be read as "separate daughter of Babylon." It needs to be seen that the word "daughter" implies a symbolic Babylon that comes later in time. We know Isaiah is not talking about ancient Babylon because of the word virgin which indicates one that is separate.

Notice also, from verse one that it is specific in speaking of the <u>daughter</u> of the Chaldeans – rather than just the Chaldeans of ancient Babylon. This proposes a similarity between the two Babylons from the words, "...O daughter of the Chaldeans..." Here's why. The Chaldeans were the devoted people of science in the ancient kingdom. They were highly thought of for solving difficult problems. In our modern era many nations have their scientists and engineers, but among all countries of the world what country is best known for its know-how? Yes, the whole world knows America is renowned for its know-how!

Students from all over the world want to come to America's universities to be educated. Russia and China are great countries too, but American know-how has helped make them more so than they otherwise would be today. For example, when Nixon was president, he made it possible for the Soviet Union to get whatever they wanted from our patent office, and when Clinton was in office, he did the same for Red China. It is no secret that the Japanese have copied our technology extensively among the more notable countries that have been helped by it.

World class know-how is such an important point in identifying America here that it is mentioned even more clearly in verse ten. Verse ten says, "...You have said, 'No one sees me,' Your wisdom and your knowledge have warped you; and you have said in your heart, 'I am and there is no one else besides me.'" The words "no one sees me" has strong overtones that the daughter of Babylon has stealth technology. If it means to be understood this way, then this would be a general "timing indicator" for when judgment will come upon her in the latter days. In other words, the ensuing period of judgment wouldn't come before she had stealth technology, but now she has it.

The words, "you have said in your heart, 'I am, and there is no one else beside me'" reveals the city-state we are analyzing believes <u>it has a technological edge</u> over all others. This is definitely true of America, but it is not true of Iraq, or Iraq's Babylon or of Rome in our end-time generation that a few have proposed as being Mystery Babylon. They do not have a technological edge over all other nations which disqualifies them as being the daughter of Babylon. So, we know this prophecy is not referring to the nations of Italy or Iraq, but it does accord with America better than any other nation to be considered as a likely candidate.

If we look again at verse one, we will see it is a general overview of the chapter in terms of the chastisement determined to come upon this country, and it tells us quite a lot. For example, the word for "come down" in the Hebrew, is "yarad" and has the connotation to bring down or to be forcibly subdued. The word "sit" has the connotation, in the Hebrew, to endure. In other words, **this chastisement is for a period of time** that will not end quickly. The word "dust" in the Hebrew, also has the connotation of ashes and rubbish. So, it has been revealed to us in just those few words that this country will be attacked and occupied for a period of time.

The next words of verse one, "sit on the ground **without a throne**" reveal the present government will be done away with. The word "throne" in the Hebrew, has the connotation of covered or protected seat of authority. This means the seat of government itself, and the agencies that protect it, will be done away with by the forces that will subdue this country.

From verse one and verse five it appears that the first two things that become evident in this chastisement of America are 1) an economic downturn and 2) what could be viewed as terrorist attacks. We read in verse one, "for you shall no longer be called tender and delicate." This implies much of this country has known an easygoing lifestyle in the past but this easy lifestyle will begin to diminish. As you know, recession, deflation, and inflation can be typical factors in an economic downturn. It is implied in this verse that something will compound and prolong this downturn.

You've probably noticed the price of food, homes and vehicles continue to go up. The price of fuel as well. This is definitely an inflationary trend.

Verse two and the first part of verse three reveal this country is invaded and occupied after the economy has been in a severe down-turn. It says, "Take the millstones and grind meal. Remove the veil, take off the skirt, uncover the thigh, pass through the rivers. Your nakedness shall be uncovered, yes, your shame will be seen."

Those words, "Take the millstones and grind meal" is the same as saying the time for conveniences and luxury is over. Prepare to do your work the hard way. It will be like turning the clock back 50 or more years. The conveniences we expect will decline. This country's problems will get worse because of war. The country will be invaded and occupied. Another way we know this is because of the words "Your nakedness shall be uncovered." The word "uncovered" in the Hebrew, has the additional connotation of being taken captive.

We must remember, that this country is trying to portray itself to the world (according to the context of this chapter) as a virgin (meaning morally justified in her role in the world), as the daughter of science (daughter of the Chaldeans), and as the lady of kingdoms. But the Lord is saying, but "your nakedness shall be uncovered." "Your nakedness" implies what this country doesn't want the world to see or know about it.

America doesn't want the world to know and believe that its fall from grace was the result of it trading its commitment to God for becoming lovers of pleasures rather than lovers of God. The words, "yes your shame will be seen" imply its disgrace. This country will not show its shame until it has been disgraced. What would disgrace America? Would it not be loss of power, loss of a vibrant economy, loss of its Constitutional freedoms, and loss of freedom of religion?

We return to the last words of verse two that say, "pass through the rivers." They are full of symbolism. But in the Hebrew here, the word "rivers" is really referring to the invading forces or armies. The word "rivers" in the Hebrew is "nehar" and comes from the root word which means to assemble to flow together – like different streams coming together to form a river. This represents and reveals, a converging of forces for a common cause. The words "pass through" come from the Hebrew word "abar" and can have the additional connotation to be carried away by. So, what this is saying is that a sizeable number of people will be forcibly displaced to locations more favorable to the occupation forces. FEMA type camps come to mind. Occupation forces will make use of these camps so conveniently available to them.

The Lord is allowing this judgment to unfold in this way because He is angry with a people who have rebelled against Him while at the same time claiming to be a Christian nation. He will no longer allow for the hypocrisy and the evil that He sees. So, we see the last part of verse three saying, "I will take vengeance, and I will not arbitrate with a man." The time to arbitrate with God is right now and it is done through repentance, submitting to the Lordship of Jesus Christ and establishing a daily relationship with Him. If this is your lifestyle, then you are in His safekeeping. If not, you have cause to be concerned.

Moving on to verse four we have <u>additional evidence</u> that this is not speaking about ancient or rebuilt Babylon. It says, "As for our Redeemer, the Lord of hosts is His Name, the Holy One of Israel. The word "Redeemer" here is the same as that used in the book of Job 19.25 where Job said, "For I know that my Redeemer lives, and He shall stand at last on the earth."

Only one has come to earth as the Redeemer of mankind and He is Jesus Christ. This prophecy is speaking about a time in which Jesus Christ is known and has been proclaimed to the world. This would not apply to historic Babylon, but it does speak of America because it was **founded** upon the Judeo-Christian religion. Ancient Babylon did not embrace Jesus Christ nor was He known to them.

The next calamity Isaiah mentions in verse five is <u>another identifier</u> for America where it says, "Sit in silence, and go into darkness, O daughter of the Chaldeans; For you shall no longer be called the Lady of kingdoms."

Daughter of the Chaldeans is being addressed here, which alludes to the scientific technologies, in particular, that drives this country's economy. America has been known as the leading industrial nation and for its high-tech manufacturing abilities. In this verse, we see the words, "sit in silence and go into darkness." This implies electrical grid problems. Manufacturing plants are very quiet when all the noisy machinery inside comes to a standstill. The lights go out leaving you to sit in the darkness.

There are several things that could bring down the electrical grid; for example, an emp attack or an act of terrorism. In Luke 21.11 Jesus said, that there will be "… fearful sights" and the Greek word there can also be translated "terrors" i.e., terrorists' acts.

Verse five also describes this country as "Lady of Kingdoms." "Lady" in the Hebrew means one who has limited authority, power and control over others. As far as control goes, America has been criticized for trying to be the world's policeman, and many foreign nations despise her in that role. She strives to have a controlling interest in other countries affairs in a variety of ways such as through most favored nation trade status and seeing other countries' currencies tied to the value of its dollar. She is called lady here, which would allude to her skills in diplomacy. America is also a leading country in providing foreign aid giving her a very controlling influence in other countries affairs.

This just simply provides further confirmation concerning this Babylon's identity of the end-time. Even though Iraq has been an important source of oil energy it has certainly not been known as the Lady of kingdoms in our present day. Modern day Rome, though she has had considerable influence many centuries ago, is definitely not the mistress of kingdoms today. Neither can she say, "I am, and there is no one else beside me," in the sense of economic, technological or military supremacy.

Some might think verse five could also apply to the Vatican. It has a lot of influence in nations that are predominately Catholic, I agree, but not a lot in Islamic countries or China, Russia, Japan North Korea etc. Neither is it known as the country of world-renowned know-how. It just doesn't meet all the necessary criteria given for identifying this Babylon here. All those identifying criteria was given by the Lord for a reason – so we wouldn't miss identifying correctly this end-time Babylon as it is mentioned here.

Now we come to verse six. It says, "I was angry with My people; I have profaned My inheritance and given the into your hand. You showed them no mercy; on the elderly you laid your yoke very heavily.

The words "I have profaned My inheritance" means for the purpose of this chastisement the Lord will now view and treat people who call themselves Christians but haven't had a born again experience, and therefore no real relationship with Him as being secular. The words, "and given them into your hand" imply giving them into the hands of an anti-Christian element. The words, "you showed then no mercy: reveal a severe backlash of persecution against them. Yes, religious persecution breaks out and it will get to be very intense. The words, "on the elderly you laid your yoke very heavily" is referring to an imposition laid upon senior citizens by its own government. It isn't clear what this is, but one thing that would sure do it would be a collapse of the social security system or an intentional devaluation of the dollar causing high inflation for people on a fixed income.

In verse seven it reveals the general time period of the daughter of Babylon we are analyzing. It says, "And you said, 'I shall be a lady forever,' So, that you did not take these things to heart, nor remember **the latter end** of them.'" So, this daughter of Babylon, of the end-time, is specified here – not historical Babylon.

In verse eight is another identifier. It says, "Therefore hear this now, you who are given to pleasures, who dwell securely, who say in your heart, 'I am, and there is no one else beside me...'"

The words, "given to" has a wide application of meanings as: pay for, charge for, yield to, and be occupied with. The word "pleasures" refers to all types of sensual gratification in the general sense.

For example, pursuing the luxuries of life, being wined and dined in fine restaurants, bungee jumping, going to Disney like parks, golfing, bingo, horse racing, yachting, surfing, boat and car racing, and the list could be made quite long. The Lord isn't condemning all types of pleasure here, but merely to point out that this end-time Babylon, in particular, **is occupied** with them providing another way we can identify who He is speaking about. Is there any other country more given to pleasures than America that also meets all the other aforementioned criteria for identifying her? I don't know of any.

Another identifier in verse eight says "who dwell securely." Americans haven't built walls around their cities. America has been a super power both militarily and economically and its Constitution has provided, up to now, important liberties that other nations are envious to have. This certainly does not apply to the Iraqis striving to have the necessities of life. Neither does this verse apply to Rome, Italy, nor the Vatican because they are not super powers as specified in this verse and the Vatican is not given to pleasures.

Verses eight and nine go on to pinpoint the uniqueness of this judgment upon the daughter of Babylon. It reads, "I shall not sit as a widow, nor shall I know the loss of children; **but these two things shall come to you in a moment, in one day:** the loss of children and widowhood. They shall come upon you in their fullness."

This is describing a very quick and dramatic reduction in the population from the words, "in a moment in one day." The word "moment' in the Hebrew, means in an instant. The Medes and Persians didn't destroy Babylon. That didn't happen until many years later under Xerxes and the Parthians. This is another reason we know it isn't speaking about historical Babylon here. Only in the twentieth and twenty-first centuries has it been possible to bring about massive destruction, in an instant, with exploding nuclear warheads. <u>This specifically underscores an end-time judgment.</u>

The Lord is quite specific about a particular aspect of this judgment starting in verse 11. He says, "Therefore evil will come upon you; you shall not know from where it arises. And trouble shall fall upon you; you will not be able to put it off. And desolation shall come upon you suddenly, which you shall not know."

The word "evil" in the Hebrew here means an **exceedingly great** calamity that leaves sorrow and trouble. The words "you shall not know from where it arises," means it comes upon you in a way you didn't expect it. The words, "you shall not be able to put it off" means there will be no way to cancel the coming calamity because it happens suddenly, and it results in desolation. I am reminded of the newest weapon – the hypersonic missile for which there seems to be no defense against it so far. The words, "which you shall not know" is like saying, "he didn't know what hit him."

One more thing to see in this verse is that it says this evil or calamity arises (to rise up), and then falls to bring about great destruction. In our modern-day vernacular, this verse could be indicating America's enemies will launch intercontinental ballistic missiles from submarines at close range to cut short any response time needed to intercept them ("You will not be able to put it off"), and it will also deny precious warning time needed for people to escape these targeted cities. Ah, you say, but this won't happen because America has an underwater sensor system to detect where enemy submarines are at all times. This is only partly true. It was deactivated under the

Clinton administration. A close friend of mine confirmed this when he quoted the following statement: "Despite wide interest in the once secret system, the Navy says it has little money for old gear for deep sea monitoring unneeded for new kinds of threats. Rear admiral James G. Prout 3d, deputy Chief of Staff of the Pacific fleet told the senate armed services committee in March that both the Pacific and Atlantic fleets were moth balling their SOSUS arrays."

Now verse fourteen describes the scene of destruction in a little more detail saying, "Behold, they shall be as stubble, the fire shall burn them, they shall not deliver themselves from the power of the flame; It shall not be a coal to be warmed by nor a fire to sit before!"

The word "burn" here in the Hebrew here can also mean direction of, ordinance and means to be set on fire, and be completely consumed by it. The word "flame" here means a bright flash from the head of. In this case we understand it to be from the warheads of missiles. We would have to agree that this is no ordinary fire. It would have been totally foreign to the ancients. This lends support to those being guided missiles, and it definitely is the kind of flame that evokes terror.

Now we come to verse 15. It says, "Thus shall they be to you with who you have labored, your merchants from your youth; They shall wander each one to his quarter. No one shall save you." This means America's so-called friends in NATO will not come to her aid. America will be abandoned – left to go it alone!

The word "Babylon" is being used to identify the woman in both the Old and New Testament passages. This is another clue that the scripture isn't referring to historical Babylon of Nebuchadnezzar or Belshazzar's day. You see the lion was always symbolical of historical Babylon not a woman. The statue of Liberty is the symbol of a woman the world over associates with America.

The use of the word "Babylon" does infer a nation is being alluded to. In both passages of Revelation and Isaiah we are viewing the moral and spiritual condition as it is, in the declining stages in the end time. The word "Babylon" means confusion. In todays society what is causing confusion? Could it be redefining what constitutes a marriage? Could it be what is known as political correctness where voicing what God says are abominations to Him are now considered hate speech? Is it putting a verbal spin on what is evil and wrong and calling it ok? Is it suppressing scientific discoveries that reveal the Bible is true after all? Is it bribing the justice system to cover up crimes of hate and greed? Is it slaughtering the unborn because they are not deemed to be human even though they have human DNA and their own fingerprints that reveal they are their own person? Do I need to make this list any longer to make this point?

I found it interesting that the word "confusion" also means "wilderness." In both cases, the woman in Isaiah and Revelation are experiencing wilderness conditions. The word "wilderness" means uncultured and uncivilized. What does uncultured imply? It implies those who are not tolerant, not given to respect, not well educated. Does this remind you of those who graduate from high school that still can't read? What about those given to rioting and violent protests? What about those who prey on the weak such as those who engage in the knockout game? What happened to respect and politeness? I believe we have a great deal of evidence that our society is becoming very uncultured.

Another thing that needs to be seen from the Revelation passage is that while the nation has declined to a wilderness condition the governing authorities have essentially fleeced the populace. The government has provided well for itself. Notice Revelation 17.4 says, "The woman was arrayed in purple and scarlet, and adorned with gold and precious stones and pearls having in her hand a golden cup full of abominations and filthiness of her fornication." I just don't see where the government has sacrificed for the people here?

I do see where government turns on its own people. In verse six it reads, "I saw the woman drunk with the blood of the saints and with the blood of the martyrs of Jesus…" In the year 2015 the Department of Homeland Security coordinated with the military (special ops) in training exercises (called Jade Helm 15) for the purpose of rounding up civilians who they would deem to be a threat to society and the government.

Are we not seeing Bible prophecy being fulfilled right before our eyes? The government has not figured the rapture of the Bride of Christ into their plans though.

The saints being killed (in Revelation 17.6) are great tribulation saints – not the Bride of Christ. So, it is important for people to realize they need to be serious about their relationship with Christ or they won't be going in the rapture. It is about to make a real difference for those who have set their affection on things above and not on the things of earth! Narrow is the way that leads to life. Few that find it!

CHAPTER TWELVE

Expectant or Unaware and The Temple

Expectant or Unaware are two diametrically opposed concepts. I use these words with regard to the return of Christ for His Church. I believe Satan would rather people be unaware of when Christ will return and that he would perpetuate the idea that the time of Christ's return is unknowable so don't be concerned about it. On the other-hand Jesus would teach that we should be expectant of His return and would point out prophetic events for His people to be watching for, so they would know when the time of His return is drawing near.

Satan is clever in promoting unawareness by having people quote Matthew 24.42. You are likely familiar with this verse. It reads, "Watch therefore, for you do not know what hour your Lord is coming." He thinks he has a shut and closed case at this point. But we really need to stop and think about the words that Jesus is using here. Let's take the first word "watch." Does it make any sense to say watch to people who are already watching or to say watch to people who aren't watching?

It is important to look at the passage this verse was taken from and the context of the passage. Jesus gave several examples here so let's look at the first one in verses 37-39. "But as the days of Noah were so also will the coming of the Son of

Man be. For as in the days before the flood, they were eating and drinking, marrying and giving in marriage until the day that Noah entered the ark, and did not know until the flood came and took them all away, so also will the coming of the Son of Man be."

The main theme Jesus is addressing in this example is that society didn't believe Noah's message or that his work was relevant to their day. They rejected the message to prepare themselves for the global change that was coming. Today society is choosing unconcern and irrelevance regarding the Word of God as well.

I had an experience years ago of what it will be like when the rapture takes place. One night I was sound asleep when, suddenly, I was awakened at 2 O'clock in the morning by the high-pitched sound of a trumpet. It was a loud unwavering tone and it was moving across the sky. I wanted my wife to hear what I was experiencing so I woke her up and said, "Do you hear that sound of a horn? And she said, "No, I don't hear anything." I said, "I don't see how you can miss it." It was then I knew this experience was from the Lord, not to teach my wife something but to teach me something. That was when I realized born again Christians have a set of spiritual ears to hear with that those spiritually dead don't have activated. That experience has certainly convinced me the rapture will be as a thief in the night.

There is a scripture in Proverbs 1.4 that I find quite interesting. It says, "Wealth is worthless in the day of wrath, but righteousness delivers from death." That day of wrath is the great tribulation time. Secondly, this verse indicates that what does have real value is righteousness, because righteousness will bring deliverance that will allow one to escape the day of wrath.

Sometimes what the scripture doesn't say can be as revealing as what it does say. For example, consider Revelation 13.8-9. It reads, "All inhabitants of the earth will worship the beast – all whose names have not been written in the book of life belonging to the Lamb that was slain from the creation of the world. He who has an ear, let him hear." What's missing here? It is the words "what the Spirit says to the churches." Why are these words missing when they were included **without exception** in chapters two and three each time one of the churches was addressed? Those words are missing in this passage because the Church is not present on earth when the statement is made, "He who has an ear, let him hear." This also tells us that God does not consider people who become saints in the great tribulation time as part of the Church. Yes, they will get to rule and reign with Christ in the millennium, but they are considered in a different category of saints from that of the Church.

Sometimes just the sequence of events can be quite revealing. For example, In Isaiah chapter 63 speaks of the day of the Lord's wrath, but in the preceding chapter 62 we can find where it speaks of saints delivered prior to that time. Notice what Isaiah 62.11-12 says: "The Lord has made proclamation to the ends of the earth: Say to the Daughter of Zion, see your Savior comes! See, His reward is with Him, and His recompense accompanies Him. They will be called the Holy People, the Redeemed of the Lord; and you will be called Sought After, The City No Longer Deserted."

The Savior's recompense is described in this verse as "the Redeemed of the Lord" in contrast to the Daughter of Zion who is called "Sought After." A definite distinction is made between the two groups. Now why is the Redeemed of the Church called His recompense? Simply because the Church, His bride compensated for the loss incurred in Israel's rejection of our Lord Jesus Christ. Why is the daughter of Zion called Sought After? Because throughout Scripture we find God has consistently sought after them rather than the Jewish people seeking after God. In case some might think His recompense are angels it needs to be pointed out angels are never called the Redeemed of the Lord. It is verse eleven that indicates a prior rapture took place sometime previous to His return here.

In this verse the Lord Himself is making a proclamation, an announcement, not just to Israel, but to the whole earth that He, the Messiah, is making His appearance to Israel as their Savior. This is exactly the way He returns at the end of the great tribulation time to stop the battle of nations being waged against Israel. Not only does the Lord make this announcement, but the Jews are also told to notice the Lord's recompense is returning **with** Him. The only way for this to be possible is they would have had to have been raptured prior to His second coning to rule and reign.

A confirming promise is given to us in Galatians 1.3-4. This passage reads, "Grace and peace to you from God our Father and the Lord Jesus Christ, who gave Himself for our sins **to rescue us** from the present evil age, according to the will of our God and Father." Paul clearly indicates this rescue is part of God's will or plan for us, His saints. The word "from" here in the Greek, means "out of." The only way to be rescued <u>out of</u> the evil age would necessitate a rapture.

Jesus' teaching is even more clear on this. In Luke chapter 21 several events are mentioned concerning the great tribulation, but when you get to verse 36 a promise of hope is given by Jesus. He says, "Watch ye therefore, and pray always, that ye may be accounted worthy to escape all these things that shall come to pass, and to stand before the Son of Man." In this Luke passage, it is indicated the believers who measure up to the criterion set by the Lord **will be exempt** from the time of great trial and judgments to come on the earth. Secondly, Jesus even indicates where the place of escape will be when He says that those who escape will stand before the Son of Man. And where is the Son of Man when the great tribulation events are occurring? We know from Revelation chapters four through six that Jesus is in heaven before the throne opening the book with the seven seals. So, to stand before the Son of Man, in heaven, <u>it requires the saints to have been translated there</u>! We need not kid ourselves, people left to face tribulation events haven't escaped them. The words of Samuel show considerable wisdom when he said that obedience is better than sacrifice.

Jesus has no intention of ruling on the earth until Israel is first dealt with, and the tribulation period (also known as Daniel's 70th week) is designed to deal with Israel. But neither is it in God's plan to let the world continue in sinful practices indefinitely, and so the great tribulation will deal with the Gentile nations also. God would not be a God of love if He didn't (at some point) bring judgment on the evil and the wicked. Yes, Psalm 110.1 will be fulfilled where it says that His enemies will be put under His feet. It is God's full intention to take the kingdoms of this world away from Satan and give them to Jesus.

Because of the promise given to the saints to escape God's time of wrath, they will be allowed to escape the coming judgments. It has nothing to do with saints today being any better in God's eyes. than saints from past generations. We just happen to be the saints who are concluding the Church age. None of the saints of any prior age has had to go through the great tribulation so why would the Church be singled out to go through it? They won't be.

The apostle Paul, in 1 Thessalonians 5.9 said, "God did not appoint us to suffer wrath but to receive salvation through our Lord Jesus Christ." The verse implies **there is an appointed time** for the completion of our salvation, and it is Jesus who will complete it. To complete our salvation implies a work of deliverance involving a final rescue act. Paul confirms this (in Romans 13.11) by saying, "The hour has come for you to wake up from your slumber, because our salvation is nearer now than when we first believed." He is saying that there is a particular time for its completion.

Paul stated that the Corinthians also held the position of expectancy. In 1 Corinthians 1.7 he said, "Therefore you do not lack any spiritual gift as you eagerly wait for our Lord Jesus Christ to be revealed. What were they waiting for? They were waiting for the Lord Jesus Christ to be revealed. There was no indication here that they were apprehensive of the coming great tribulation period.

The beginning of Revelation chapter four opens with John being caught up to heaven in the vicinity of God's throne where he makes some very interesting observations. In verse four it reads, "Surrounding the throne were twenty-four other thrones, and seated on them were twenty-four elders. They were dressed in white and had crowns of gold on their heads." Now we also need to read Revelation 1.5-6 to help us unlock the meaning of what we are viewing. It says, To Him who loves us and had freed us from our sins by His blood and has made us to be a kingdom and priests to serve His God and Father to Him be glory and power for ever and ever!"

The part which is significant to us is the part indicating the redeemed are a priesthood unto God. From the Old Testament we learn that there are 24 orders of the priesthood, and this was also a type of the new. So, the 24 elders seen in Revelation represented the fulness of the priesthood being present before the throne of God. John sees the point in time when the priesthood is finally complete before God not just partially complete. This indicated then that all the redeemed (the Church) being present before the throne of God.

Secondly, they are seen with crowns on their heads. We know the saints don't receive their crowns until after they are translated **and all at the same time.** Paul indicates this in 2 Timothy 4.8. He said, "Now there is in store for me the crown of righteousness, which the Lord, the righteous Judge, will award to me on that day- and not only to me, but also to all who have longed for His appearing."

Yes, Paul knew he would receive a crown, but not immediately after he died. He must wait for **the appointed time** – until the crowns are awarded to all the Church saints. John, in heaven, sees the future when the elders have crowns, so this reveals to us the particular time period finally arrives when all the saints receive their crowns.

Now the crowned elders are seen in chapter four before the antichrist is revealed in chapter six. The very sequence of these events, therefore, supports the rapture of the Church as being pre-tribulation.

The Jerusalem Temple

Scripture indicates the temple in Jerusalem will be built again during this 1948 generation (Matthew 24.15; 2 Thessalonians 2.4), but the question has been, will the temple be built before or during the tribulation? I believe we have enough evidence from Scripture to be able to say the Church will not be here to see the building of the Jewish temple in Jerusalem.

One big clue comes from Daniel 9.27 in which the Antichrist confirms the covenant with Israel. There will be little to no opposition confirming this covenant because of a temple probably because it won't exist yet. But a little less than three and a half years later we will see strong opposition by the Antichrist to the altar sacrifices.

It is becoming increasingly obvious that the Jews plan to build their temple on the temple mount probably just north of the Dome of the Rock. We have an inference to this from Revelation 11.2. It infers this as it says, "Leave out the court which is outside the temple, and do not measure it for it has been given to the nations..." (NASV). Some have proposed that Jerusalem should be declared an international city as a resolution between Moslems and Jews with regard to the temple mount. So, if there isn't room for the court of the Gentiles this may be due to the temple being situated too close to the Dome of the Rock.

Now here is where it gets interesting. Due to all the events that have transpired over the centuries the Jewish Sanhedrin considers that area of the temple mount unclean and that it must therefore be cleansed before any building can commence. In turn, they will build an altar for sacrifices to cleanse the temple mount before any building is allowed. This altar of sacrifice has now been built and is ready to be put into use. There is a precedent from past history. When the Babylonian Jews returned from Babylon, they first built an altar for burnt offerings before they started building the temple again (Ezra 3.2, 6). It should also be noted that the Jews now have at least two red heifers that meet the requirements of the law for being sacrificed on this altar.

We must now go to Daniel 8.13-14 to complete the end-time picture here. This passage reads, "...How long will the vision be, <u>concerning the daily sacrifices</u> and the transgression of desolation, the giving of both the sanctuary and the host to be trampled underfoot? "And he said to me, "For two thousand three hundred days <u>then the sanctuary will be cleansed</u>." This period is equivalent to six years, four months, and twenty days that closes out the seventieth week.

Since this will occur in the seven-year tribulation period we must subtract the six years, four months, and twenty days from seven years to find out when the priesthood will begin offering sacrifices. This leaves seven months and ten days into the seven-year period before the daily sacrifices are offered. Therefore, the implication is they <u>won't</u> begin building the temple until shortly after this <u>in the first year</u> of the seven-year tribulation. It is interesting that this temple will also be built in troublesome times as was the one in Ezra's time (Daniel 9.25; Ezra 4.4).

CHAPTER THIRTEEN

WAR OF EZEKIEL 38 AND 39 VERSUS ARMAGEDDON

Preparation for the battle of Armageddon occurs under the sixth bowl judgment (Revelation 16.12-14. 16). "Then the sixth angel poured out his bowl on the great river Euphrates, and its water was dried up, so that the way of the kings from the east might be prepared. And I saw three unclean spirits like frogs coming out of the mouth of the dragon, out of the mouth of the beast, and out of the mouth of the false prophet. For they are spirits of demons, performing signs, which go out to the kings of the earth, and to the whole world, to gather them to the battle of that great day of God Almighty. [v.16] And they gathered them together to the place called in Hebrew, Armageddon.

    I am convinced <u>from scripture</u> that the war mentioned in Ezekiel 38 and 39, and the war of Armageddon are the same war. Why? They are both described as being the final conflict before Jesus reigns as King on earth. So, if they weren't the same war then one of them couldn't be the final conflict, and that would pose a problem in the timing. The accounts have eerie similarities, but also each account provides unique information just as the accounts in Matthew, Mark and Luke did relative to each other.

For example, in Ezekiel 38 are listed specific nations involved in the battle against Israel but it doesn't list them all. Verse nine says, "You will ascend, coming like a storm, covering the land like a cloud, you and all your troops <u>and many peoples</u> with you." So there will be other nations involved. Then it is from Daniel chapter eleven and verse 44 that we find the antichrist has enemies outside of Israel and they are coming to eliminate the antichrist. That is why the antichrist positions himself in Israel hoping the remaining Jews will be killed in this great conflict at that time.

Daniel 11.44-45, a passage that alludes to these reads, "But news from the east and the north shall trouble him; therefore, he shall go out with great fury to destroy and annihilate many. And he shall plant the tents of his palace between the seas and the glorious holy mountain; yet he shall come to his end, and no one will help him."

Now view similarities for the Ezekiel war and Armageddon. Both accounts mention a very great earthquake. Ezekiel 38.19-20 reads, "For in My jealousy and in the fire of My wrath I have spoken. 'Surely in that day there shall be a great earthquake in the land of Israel, so that the fish of the sea, the birds of the heavens, the beasts of the field, all creeping things that creep upon the earth, and all men who are on the face of the earth shall shake at My presence. The mountains shall be thrown down, the steep places shall fall, and every wall shall fall to the ground."

Now under the seventh bowl judgment when the war of Armageddon rages, Revelation 16.18,20 reads, "And there were noises and thunderings and lightnings; and there was <u>a great earthquake</u>, such a mighty and great earthquake, as had not occurred since men were on the earth. Then every island fled away and the mountains were not found."

Besides the similarity of the two earthquake accounts there is the problem with the mountains being thrown down. If the mountains are thrown down in the Ezekiel account, then there shouldn't still be mountains to be thrown down at the time of the battle of Armageddon. Therefore, the timing of these battles is the same.

The next similarity are great hailstones. Ezekiel 38.22 reads, "And I will bring him to judgment with pestilence and blood shed; I will rain down on him, on his troops, and on the many peoples who are with him flooding rain, <u>great hailstones</u>, fire and brimstone."

In Revelation 16.21 (still under the 7th bowl judgment) it reads, "And great hail from heaven fell upon men, each hailstone about the weight of a talent. Men blasphemed God because of the plague of the hail, since that plague was exceedingly great."

The next similarity is God's sacrificial meal for the birds and the beasts. Ezekiel 39.17-18, 20 reads, "And as for you Son of Man, thus says the Lord God, speak to every sort of bird and to every beast of the field; assemble yourselves and come; gather together from all sides to My sacrificial meal which I am sacrificing for you, a great sacrificial meal on the mountains of Israel, that you may eat flesh and drink blood. You shall eat the flesh of the mighty, drink the blood of the princes of the earth...[v.20] You shall be filled at My table with horses, and riders, with mighty men and with all the men of war, says the Lord God."

In Revelation 19.17-18 it says, "Then I saw an angel standing in the sun; and he cried with a loud voice, saying to all the birds that fly in the midst of heaven, 'come and gather together for the supper of the great God, that you may eat the flesh of kings, the flesh of captains, the flesh of mighty men, the flesh of horses and of those who sit on them, and the flesh of all people, free and slave, both small and great."

After God retaliates against the armies fighting against Israel, He makes a statement (Ezekiel 39.7) and says, "So I will make My holy name known in the midst of My people Israel and I will not let them profane My holy name anymore. <u>Then the nations shall know that I am the LORD, the Holy One in Israel</u>." This statement convinces me that the war described here in Ezekiel 38 and 39 is the last war, that of Armageddon, from that phrase, "I will not let them profane My holy name anymore."

To understand this, we need to understand the word "profane." So, how would one profane the name of the Lord? And what does that mean? First of all, it would be some kind of outward manifestation and in this case it would most likely be verbal and could be followed by a gesture such as a frown, a shaking of the head, or just walking away from discussing the Lord. Have you ever noticed that when a Jewish person is discussing religion in any way that he avoids the name of Jesus crossing his lips? He may say Messiah, or Yeshua but almost never the name of Jesus. You see if they would acknowledge the name of Jesus, by its own meaning that of Savior, they won't acknowledge that.

So, according to the last phrase – <u>not</u> profaning the name of the Lord would mean the nations <u>would then know</u> that Jesus is acknowledged as Lord by the very nation that should be acknowledging it. That was one purpose for the nation of Israel (Exodus 19.5-6; Isaiah 49.6).

Now let's go to the triumphal entry (Luke 19.28-44). The disciples following Jesus were voicing praise to Jesus when some of the Pharisees cried out to Jesus to rebuke them. Why? Because they considered it blasphemy that He should receive praise only meant for God. Then in verse 41 it says, "Now as He drew near, He saw the city and wept over it." And in verse 44 the reason is given; "…because you did not know the time of your visitation." This was prophesied by Isaiah in chapter 53 verse three. It says, "He is despised by men, a man of sorrows and acquainted with grief and we hid as it were our faces from Him; He was despised, and we did not esteem Him." So, what part of the definition of "profane" was this? We recognize it as sorrow, and was it verbal? Yes. Was He heartbroken (another definition of sorrow)? Yes. Did His heart feel wounded? Yes. And on the cross He heart was even pierced (one definition of profane meaning to "bore" into).

Now let's go to one of the primary definitions of the word profane which is, to break one's word. Well, what was the covenant word that Israel was to keep? When asked what the greatest commandment was, Jesus replied (in Matthew 22.37) "You shall love the Lord your God with all your heart, with all your soul, and with all your mind." So Israel broke this commandment when they had Jesus crucified. You don't crucify someone if you love them only if you hate them. So, by not loving Jesus as Lord and God, Israel has profaned His great name! The last similarity ties into this when Jesus Himself returns where He is visibly seen.

Revelation 19.11-16, 19 reads, "Now I saw heaven opened and behold a white horse. And He who sat on him was called Faithful and True, and in righteousness He judges and makes war. His eyes were like a flame of fire, and on His head were many crowns. He had a name written that no one knew except Himself. He was clothed with a robe dipped in blood, and His name is called the Word of God. And the armies in heaven, clothed in fine linen, white and clean followed Him on white horses. Now out of His mouth goes a sharp sword, that with it He should strike the nations. And He Himself will rule with a rod of iron. He Himself treads the winepress of the fierceness and wrath of Almighty God. And He has on His robe and on His thigh a name written; KING of KINGS and LORD of LORDS. [v.19] And I saw the beast, the kings of the earth, and their armies gathered together to make war against Him who sat on the horse and against His army."

Then in Ezekiel 38.23 it says, "Thus I will magnify Myself, and I will be known **in the eyes** of many nations. Then they shall know that I am the Lord." In Ezekiel 39.7 we read earlier the phrase, "the nations shall know that I am the Lord the Holy One **in Israel**." Yes, Jesus will be visibly seen at this time, and reveals Himself to the whole world in great glory!

These are the reasons the war mentioned in Ezekiel 38 and 39 will not happen for several years yet and that it is the same war as Armageddon. The war going on with Israel now will probably be the war that concludes with the antichrist confirming a covenant of peace with Israel.

CHAPTER FOURTEEN

CHERISHED SECRET REVEALED

One might not think of the book Song of Solomon as containing any prophetic verses but chapter two intimates a prophetic voice. Verse one is a clue that there is something special to take note of when it says, "I am the rose of Sharon, and the lily of the valleys." Where have we seen those first two words before – "I am?" They appeared in Exodus 3.14, "And God said to Moses, I AM WHO I AM. And He said, thus you shall say to the children of Israel, 'I AM has sent me to you." So the typology of the first verse ("I am the rose of Sharon") reveals this is speaking of Jesus. In the book of Revelation chapter 22 the words "I am" are used five times and three of those are associated with the phrase "I am coming quickly."

From the typology of Song of Solomon chapter two and verse four we realize there is a love affair taking place between Jesus and His bride to be. "He brought me to the banqueting house and His banner over me was love." Yes, she arrives at a very special place.

Beginning in verse eight we see some of the specifics of how this took place and when. I won't quote verses eight and nine but the gist is that when Jesus came, He came quickly. And then in verse ten we get to the how it happened. "My beloved spoke, and said to me, 'Rise up, my love, my fair one and come away.'" Does this remind you of what takes place at the time of the rapture? First Thessalonians 4.16 says, "For the Lord Himself will descend from heaven with a shout with the voice of an arch angel..." and [v.17] we shall be caught up.

In Song of Solomon 2.14 we see why it was easy for Jesus to select His bride-to-be to go away with Him. "O my dove, in the clefts of the rock..." She was already found to be abiding in the Rock. Jesus, Himself, said in Matthew 16.18 that He is the Rock that His Church would be established upon.

The next line of verse 14 is translated best in the KJV. It reads, "...in the secret of the stairs." Yes, this verse indicates that she was abiding in the Rock in the secret place of the stairs. So, she was expecting and waiting for the call to ascend upwards. Where did we encounter the secret of the stairs before? It was in Genesis 28. 12 and 17 where Jacob saw in a dream a ladder going from earth to heaven with the angels ascending and descending on it, and when Jacob awoke he said, "...this is the gate of heaven."

Once this secret corridor is traversed, we see in Song of Solomon 2.14 what the expectation of the bride – to – be is, "...Let me see your face, let me hear your voice..." **Verses 11-14 reveals the timing of the year this love encounter takes place.** "For lo, the winter is past, the rain is over and gone, and the voice of the turtle-dove is heard in our land. The fig tree puts forth her green figs and the vines with the tender grapes..."

It happens the turtledove is migratory and returns to Israel as early as mid-April. The fig tree puts forth the taqsh (the early fig) from late March to April. The NKJV says the vines are producing tender grapes but this is a poor translation because the vines are actually blossoming and that is where this fragrance is coming from as indicated in the NASV translation. The point is, the vines also blossom in early spring.

The spring activity just mentioned occurs in the Jewish month Abib which just happens to be in the same month of harvest as the Feast of Unleavened Bread and the Feast of Firstfruits. At the end of the time given in verses 11-13 these words are repeated, "...Rise up my love, my fair one and come away."

In the book of John chapter 14 verses 1-3 we read of the promise that Jesus Himself gave. "Let not your heart be troubled; you believe in God, believe also in Me. In My Father's house are many mansions; if it were not so, I would have told you. I go to prepare a place for you. And if I go and prepare a place for you, I will come again and <u>receive you to Myself</u>, that where I am there you may be also."

CHAPTER FIFTEEN

THE SIGNIFICANCE OF THE TWO WITNESSES

Seventy weeks as mentioned by the angel to Daniel were to be fulfilled and all those weeks have been fulfilled but the last one. The time clock to fulfill them stopped when Israel rejected Christ. So, this postponement allowed for the Church age to be ushered in. The mysterious two witnesses (of Revelation chapter eleven) will begin their ministry during the first part of the seventieth week.

If one were to draw a timeline and mark it off in seven equal increments, each representing a year, this would depict the seventieth week or seven-year tribulation period. Within the fourth increment, of our timeline, we would come to the middle of the seven-year period. So, what starts the time clock for this seven-year period? If you say it is Jesus opening the first of the seven seals allowing the rider on the white horse to be revealed and confirm a peace covenant with Israel you are right. Now what ends the seven-year period? If you say, according to Daniel 9.24 that it is after Jesus comes back with His saints and is anointed by the high priest in Jerusalem with the special anointing oil to be King of Israel you would be correct again.

It is important to establish end points for the seventieth week. Jesus takes rightful and legal claim to the throne of

David when He is anointed King by the high priest. This priest will likely be among those who flee into the wilderness for 1260 days until it is safe to return to Jerusalem. Since 1260 days is equal to three and one half Jewish years we know the religious Jews flee to the wilderness in the middle of the seven-year period and we come to a scripture that is central to our understanding and it is Daniel 12.11. The verse reads, "And from the time that the daily sacrifice is taken away, and the abomination of desolation is set up, there shall be one thousand two hundred and ninety days." So, if you count back from the end of the seven-year period 1290 days you arrive thirty days **before** completing the first three- and one-half years.

Why is this important to us? The two witnesses were given power for the duration of the 1260 days of their ministry to kill their enemies by fire (Revelation 11.3-5). Satan isn't about to let his key player (the antichrist) go up in smoke, so he waits until he knows the days of their ministry has ended before he kills the two witnesses and then he can stop the daily sacrifices without being opposed by them.

Here is where it gets interesting. You see the two witnesses were killed just before the sacrifices were stopped which will be thirty days before you begin the second three- and one-half year period of the seven years. But the two witnesses were given a ministry for a full three- and one-half years or 1260 days. So, the question is, when did their ministry start? Their ministry must therefore start at least thirty days before the Antichrist is revealed, just before the seventieth week begins. Therefore, this tells us the two witnesses appear on the world scene thirty days **before** the Antichrist does – yes, before the seven-year tribulation begins.

It is most interesting to see the two witnesses arrive in Israel sometime after the rapture of the Church to begin witnessing because the Church won't be here to do it. Who are the two witnesses? I used to think they would be Enoch and Elijah, but the Bible codes say they are Moses and Elijah. That makes sense since Enoch was a Gentile not a Jew.

It appears the focus of the two witness's ministry was on the youth because Malachi 4.5-6 declares, "Behold I will send you Elijah the prophet **before** the coming of the great and dreadful day of the Lord. And he will turn the hearts of the children to their fathers…" This would lend some support to why the 144,000 were virgins.

CHAPTER SIXTEEN

IDENTIFYING MYSTERY BABYLON, THE GREAT

In the book of Revelation chapter seventeen we find what could be described as a prophetic parable revealing unique criteria that points to the identification of Mystery Babylon. The key to understanding chapter seventeen is to view it as parenthetical. We need to under-stand it does not focus on a new sequence of events as though continuing from chapter sixteen.

You see, in the chapters prior to chapter seventeen, John has been shown the seal judgments, the trumpet judgments, and the bowl judgments. Once the judgment events have been decreed, the angel begins to show John additional information that focuses on Mystery Babylon in particular.

Verse one of chapter seventeen reads, "Then one of the seven angels who had the seven bowls came and talked with me, 'Come, I will show you the judgment of the great harlot who sits on many waters.' [v.5] And on her forehead a name was written: MYSTERY BABYLON THE GREAT, THE MOTHER OF HARLOTS AND OF THE ABOMINATIONS OF THE EARTH.'"

Mystery Babylon turns out to be a metonym for America. The word "MYSTERY" in the Greek here, means secret communiques that are religious and political in nature, passed down through secret protocol. There is a strong inference that those controlling the strings of government in the past as well as at the time of this judgment are involved with secret protocol. That means there are those appointed to government positions who have a different allegiance than to the Constitution of the United States. An example would be the people who are members of the Council on Foreign Relations whose real aim is for a one world government, and to get there one must find ways to get around the Constitution.

We now come to another even more important identifier. The word "GREAT" in "BABYLON THE GREAT" in the Greek is "mega" and means SUPER. This means **this endtime Babylon** will be known as a super entity or super power to the world just before being judged. <u>If there is any one thing which identifies America here, it is this</u>!

The little partially restored Babylon in Iraq does not fit this description, nor does the Vatican or Rome. It is a known fact; The United States has been known as a superpower among nations.

In verse one, the harlot is described as one who "sits on many waters." This is symbolism, which describes a nation made up of immigrants as the U.S. is. These identifiers are unique in that **all** of them fit the description of the U.S.

The U.S. was in a decline phase prior to 2016. Consider that in March of 2001 there was a pronounced downturn in the economy that caused bankruptcies of large corporations and hundreds of thousands of layoffs. Then in September terrorists' attacks caused the collapse of the World Trade Center, considerable destruction at the Pentagon, and the anthrax mail problem. In 2002 there were massive fires in Arizona (spread out over 50 miles in length), the 500,000-acre Biscuit fire in the Siskiyou National Forest, and severe flooding in the Midwest. In 2003 there were serious blackouts in nine states and Canada followed by hurricane Isabel (one of the worst to hit the East coast in years), also noticeable devaluation of the dollar, and the destruction of roughly 3200 homes by fire in California. Beginning in March of 2004 fuel prices took a dramatic increase at the pump. Airline fares were also affected because of this. Then in 2005 there were hurricanes Katrina, Wilma, and Rita leaving over $115 billion dollars in damages and over 1500 lives lost.

In 2006 the housing bubble began collapsing and in 2007 the U.S. dollar dropped to a new low against the Euro and the housing bubble continued its downward slide. In 2008 large mega banks began declaring huge losses. This resulted in several large bank mergers. In the same year, there was also hurricane Ike leaving $19.3 billion dollars in damages and 103 deaths. There was also a swarm of fierce tornadoes that swept across the Midwest. Auto companies GM and Chrysler required bailouts to keep solvent.

In 2009 unemployment went from 5.8% to over 10% and over 140 banks failed that year. In 2010 there was the worst oil spill in the Gulf in American history. In 2011 a very rare 5.8 earthquake hit the east coast and a deadly category five tornado hit Joplin Missouri killing over 100 people. In 2012 hurricane Sandy hit the east coast and was the second most costly storm in U.S. history. This is also the year Americans re-elected a President who ran up the national debt to over sixteen trillion dollars. In 2013 Colorado lost over four hundred homes to wildfires.

In 2001 regular unleaded gas was selling for $1.00 a gallon and in 2013 for $3.45 a gallon. Diesel had been selling for $.91 a gallon and in 2013 for $3.79 a gallon.

Skipping ahead to July of 2021 up to June of 2022 it is interesting that there have been over 100 food producers and food processing plants that have been documented as being destroyed. I don't know that this has ever happened in any other administration. Here are a few examples: In 2/5/22 the Wisconsin River Meats processing facility was destroyed by fire in Mauston, Wisconsin. In 2/15/22 Bonanza Meat Company goes up in flames in El Paso, Texas. In 2/15/22 Shearer's Foods processing plant explodes in Hermiston, Oregon. In 3/4/22 644,000 chickens destroyed at egg farm in Cecil, Maryland. In 3/10/22 915,000 chickens were destroyed at an egg farm in Taylor, Iowa. In 3/14/22 2,750,000 chickens were destroyed at an egg farm in Jefferson, Wisconsin. In 3/17/22 5,347,500 chickens destroyed at an egg farm in Buena Vista, Iowa. These are only a few from a long list. But I think it is obvious one can see what is happening here.

Mismanagement of political power will have a devastating affect on a society. Why does the U.S. give $400 million to the World Health Organization every year? Why give billions to Ukraine in the war with Russia and not be concerned about our own borders? Why sell oil from the our strategic oil reserves to Red China who threatens genocide against America?

God does not want America to go through terrible judgment. This is why the chastising events have been very measured up until now. God keeps looking for repentant hearts, so He can mitigate the judgment, but He is finding increasing rebellion against Him. This has been apparent through an increasing corrupt judicial system, perversion expressed in Hollywood films and actors, the bias in the media against morality, inequality of justice, and distaste in our public education system for any who would acknowledge God and His role in our society just to name a few examples.

As we saw earlier, the angel, speaking to John said, "Come here, I will show you the judgment of the great harlot..." and then in verse three it says, "and he carried me away in the Spirit into a wilderness and I saw a woman sitting on a scarlet beast, full of blasphemous names, having seven heads and ten horns."

The words that describe her sitting on the beast shows she has chosen to associate herself with the beast, and in return the beast is giving her its support temporarily. For a while there is a mutually agreed relationship between them, but this will change.

What we are looking at here is the United States after it has gone through a decline and pre-judgment phase. Revelation 17.4 stresses the spiritual condition of the woman showing how depraved she has become. It says, "The woman was arrayed in purple and scarlet, and adorned with gold and precious stones and pearls, having in her hand a golden cup full of abominations and the filthiness of her fornication." The fact that she is holding a cup made of gold reveals how much she cherishes what has been put into it. It is very clear that she has been a participant of what is found to be in the cup, which is abominations and filth of her fornication.

"Abominations" mean that which is detestable to God. For example, abortion is an abomination to God. The woman has come to a point where she has no shame. Her fornication is not hidden because the filthiness of it can be seen. Fornication here, represents moral depravity and the pursuit of selfish gain.

Now look at a very profound and sobering statement made in verse six. "I saw the woman drunk with the blood of the saints and with the blood of the martyrs of Jesus. And when I saw her, I marveled with great astonishment." The word "marveled" here in the Greek means astonished or flabbergasted – in this case, that there were martyrs of Jesus found here. Think about that. Severe persecution emerges in America. In our present day we are beginning to see more resistance against Church beliefs, and it is even sanctioned through some government-controlled entities. This isn't the end of the story as God will repay those persecutors big time!

It is easy to see now why the cup the woman was holding was so full of abominations and the filth of her fornication. She simply allowed any semblance or reference to God to be purged from public life. Eventually, most Christian influence will be forcibly suppressed, and martyrdoms will follow as the scripture has already indicated in verse six.

Directing our attention to verse seven, and the first part of verse eight the angel says, "Why did you marvel? I will tell you the mystery of the woman and of the beast that carries her, which has the seven heads and the ten horns. The beast that you saw was and is not and will ascend out of the bottomless pit and go to perdition."

This beast is a bit of a mystery because it has two aspects to it. The first aspect of it is a spirit that is demonic in its nature. We know this because the verse says it ascends out of the bottomless pit. This spirit of Satan will be the spirit controlling the beast. Secondly, he will eventually possess an ungodly human vessel when the right time comes to do this. This person will be known as the antichrist.

So, for the moment, the beast that John sees is representing past kingdoms, the one present in his day, and a future one as this spirit of Satan has been active in every age. We know this because of the seven heads of the beast also represent seven kings. The angel says in verse ten, "Five have fallen, one is, and the other has not yet come." This confirms that only the demonic spirit aspect of the beast could and does span the great time periods involved here.

This demonic spirit has been previously identified in Revelation 12.3 and verse 9. There it says, "Another sign appeared in heaven: behold a great fiery red dragon having seven heads and ten horns, and seven diadems on his heads. [v.9] So, the great dragon was cast out, that serpent of old, called the Devil and Satan, who deceives the whole world he was cast to the earth, and his angels were cast out with him."

So, Satan is being represented in this way to show us that he was the one who influenced world kingdoms in ages past, and who it is that will affect the judgment to come upon America, and what the end result of that influence will end up being.

In Revelation 17.8, when the angel says that the beast will ascend out of the bottomless pit and go into perdition, he doesn't mean that Satan is there now. Rather, the angel is revealing that there will be a terminating event, at the appointed time, that will cut off his ability and authority to influence mankind on the earth. Revelation 20.7-9 reveals at the conclusion of the one-thousand-year reign of Christ that Satan then comes out of the bottomless pit and tries to initiate the final battle of Gog and Magog. He miserable fails after which he is cast into the lake of fire (v.10).

The biggest mystery about the beast is when the angel (in Revelation 17.8) says, "...the beast that was, and is not, and yet is." <u>The angel is speaking of already knowing what the final outcome is</u>. Consider that the beast is described where each of its heads represent world empires. In verse ten, the angel reveals five of the seven had already fallen in history and John was living in the sixth. The Roman empire, the sixth one, would be divided into East and West, the division becoming a mortal wound that would contribute to its demise. Knowing that this would happen the angel declares that it "is not."

A seventh head or king is left to emerge in the **end time** that we understand will be of relatively short duration. This seventh head is believed to be forming now from a part of the former Roman empire.

Another point of interest is found in verse eight. It reads, "And those who dwell on the earth will marvel, whose names are not written in the Book of Life from the foundation of the world, <u>when they see the beast...</u>" Pause just a moment. Did you notice that **those observing and marveling at the beast are the lost (those whose names are not written in the Book of Life)?** The saints are conspicuously absent! We will see why before we get to the end of the chapter. In the meantime, we are provided even more information that helps identify the woman in verse nine. It says, "Here is the mind which has wisdom. The seven heads are seven mountains on which the woman sits."

This is the verse many scholars point to, me included (formerly), to say this must be speaking of Rome. They say that Rome is the city which sits on seven hills. Well, it does, but that isn't what the verse says. It says that the woman sits on seven mountains. The question we need to ask is, "would the Greek word for mountains be used if hills were really meant?" We have a precedent in Luke 3.5 where we find the word mountain and the word hill both used in the same sentence. It reads, "Every valley shall be filled, and every mountain and hill brought low..."

The Greek word for "mountain" here is "oros" just like in Revelation 17.9, but the Greek word for "hill" is "bounos." This lets us know that the word "hill" was not the intended word in Revelation 17.9 and it is an important clue that rules Rome out of the picture here.

The seven mountains in verse nine are representing seven notable kingdoms of the past and the future. This isn't the first time that a mountain has been used to represent a great kingdom. Jeremiah 51.24-25 gives us an example. In verse 24 it speaks of Babylon and in verse twenty-five the Lord goes on to say, "Behold I am against you O destroying mountain." Another example, is Daniel 2.35 where it says, "… And the stone that struck the image became a great mountain and filled the whole earth." The kingdom that it is speaking of here is the kingdom of our Lord Jesus Christ.

In Revelation 17.10 we see that these seven mountains are also linked to seven kings and in John's time, five had fallen, one was, and one was still to come. Those mountain kingdoms were Egypt, Assyria, Babylon, Medo-Persia, Greece, Rome, and revived Rome. So, what does it mean for the woman to be sitting on the seven mountain kingdoms? It means she has a prominent and residing influence in the realm of what were those kingdom empires with one present exception and that is about to change.

How are these past kingdoms known today? The Egyptian kingdom is known today as Egypt. The U.S. has a small military presence in Egypt, an embassy in Cairo, and has provided $1.557 billion in foreign aid although that amount probably varies. The heart of the Assyrian and Babylonian kingdoms is known as the nation of Iraq today. The U.S. has a much smaller presence in Iraq now, and an embassy in Baghdad, and has provided it $1.68 billion in foreign aid each year. The heart of the Grecian kingdom is the nation of Greece today. The U.S. has a military base in Crete, Grece, an embassy in Athens and they have received foreign aid through U.S. donations to the IMF. The heart of the Roman kingdom is known today as Italy. The U.S. has a military base there and an embassy in Rome, but I've left the Persian kingdom until now as this is the exception I mentioned earlier. The heart of this kingdom is known as the nation of Iran today. The U.S. only has a virtual embassy there and gives it no foreign aid. I believe this is about to change where the U.S. will soon be involved in a war with Iran making its presence felt very strongly there. The U.S. will try to bring Iran in line with a policy less threatening to the world.

And then there is the seventh kingdom – the revival of the Roman kingdom. The U.S. has embassies in every one of those nations and does extensive trade with them. In addition, nearly every country of the world has had to use the American dollar as the world reserve currency up until recently. Truly, America has made its presence felt around the world in a way no other country has.

There is another important identifier for America in verse fifteen. It says, "The waters which you saw, where the harlot sits, are peoples, multitudes, nations and tongues." The angel makes it clear; Mystery Babylon is made up of many peoples of many different tongues i.e., immigrants from many different countries. But also, within her borders are nations. This is true of all the Indian races such as the Apache nation, the Sioux nation, the Navajo nation and on and on we could list them. This certainly describes America, but it doesn't Rome, the Vatican or Iraq.

Verse ten reveals something to us about timing. The true nature of the ten kings reveal they are very anti-American. It reads, "And the ten horns which you saw, <u>and the beast</u> these will hate the harlot and make her desolate..." (NASV). This shows the Antichrist will be involved in America's downfall. It also shows America's downfall is ongoing right into the seven-year tribulation itself. This means Christians will not be here to see the complete downfall of this country. It means our departure time is drawing very near.

It should be pointed out that chapter seventeen is not the first time Babylon the Great is mentioned in Revelation. Babylon the Great is also mentioned in chapter fourteen and verse eight. There it says, "Babylon the Great is fallen, is fallen that great city because she has made all nations drink of the wine of the wrath of her fornication."

Chapters twelve, thirteen, and fourteen of Revelation represents the midpoint of the seven-year tribulation period. One way we know this, is verse nine, when people are warned not to take the mark of the beast mentioned in chapter thirteen. Chapter thirteen verse five reveals there are only three- and one-half years remaining of the seven. The important thing to see is the proclamation; that at this point in time, Babylon the Great is declared to have fallen. So, what this confirms or tells us is that after being halfway through the tribulation it reveals America is under occupation by foreign forces.

The next statement made to John, in Revelation seventeen and verse fourteen takes John ahead to the end of the Great Tribulation time. This reveals to John why the ten horns or kings give all their power and authority to the beast. It reads, "These will make war with the Lamb, and the Lamb will overcome them, for He is Lord of Lords and King of Kings, and those who are with Him are called, chosen, and faithful." So, when Jesus comes back, this verse reveals, He will wage war on this ungodly world order and His main focus, initially at His return will be upon the beast and the ten kings.

Now if you remember from verse eight it was mentioned that those observing the beast were the unsaved. So where were the saints? Here we have the answer to that in the last half of verse fourteen, which says, "and those who are with Him, are called, chosen, and faithful." The saints are already found to be with the Kings of Kings **as He returns** to wage war on the ungodly system!

There is a phrase in Revelation 17.16 – one word actually – that I find very interesting. The phrase is, "…these will hate the harlot, make her desolate…" and "make" is the word of interest. In the Greek it signifies a counter action implying to "avenge" i.e. for something America caused to happen, to them, and they want revenge.

What is happening in the world right now that is causing international turmoil? The one thing that stands out, at the moment, is an on-going currency war, and to some extent limited tariffs. Nation's central banks are devaluing currencies, so their country's exports will not be curtailed. This allows businesses to maintain jobs and keep people employed but it comes with a terrible side effect; higher and higher inflation and if it progresses long enough nations end up with civil unrest and when it can't be corrected then you have insurrections against governments and blood flows in the streets. This is exactly what is happening under the second seal of the rider on the red horse in Revelation chapter six. America also has a huge bond market bubble which is about to collapse, and a lot of foreign nations have purchased those bonds. So, when America defaults on her bonds no one gets their investment back and that doesn't sit will with investors especially foreign countries such as China, Japan and Russia.

There is a *conclusive* reason given in verse eighteen for excluding Rome as Mystery Babylon. "And the woman whom you saw is that great city which reigns over the kings of the earth." The translators could also have written the words "is to come" for the word "is" as the Greek word "esti" can mean both, "is" or "is to come." Knowing what we know from identifying Mystery Babylon as America thus far, the words "is to be" makes more sense. So, the point the angel was making is the city-state he was referring to **didn't even exist yet** in the world at the time he was speaking to John! In that case, the angel wasn't referring to Rome. Yes, at this point America was indeed a mystery!

It is important to note that ***all the clues*** given by the angel must fit to identify the woman not just some of the clues. Only America meets the criterion of all of them!

CHAPTER SEVENTEEN

THE ABOMINABLE TREND OF AMERICA

Revelation chapter seventeen shows how abominable America got to be before she is judged! When you continuously fund corruption, it grows and spreads like a cancer. We are seeing how corrupt Washington DC. Is – its bureaucracy and the agencies that are under it. The rot isn't only found there but extends to our liberal institutions as the primary source where the decay process began and flourished. These liberal institutions have brainwashed the minds of generations to believe God is irrelevant to the soundness of a society.

One of the first things these institutions did was disavow that God was the Creator of this earth and that it came about through evolutionary processes. Accountability to God gradually went out the window. Then came along the revisionists who rewrote much of our history in that they left out of the historical account references made to God and His providence in the lives of those prominent people who led our country, and the credit they gave to God for the positive outcomes they had experienced. The minds of the people must be dulled you know.

Next, the door opened wide for sexual immorality to have free reign in our society. Unmarried people began living together and skipped the marriage vows. So, you don't have the stigma for what it is – fornication – it is just called domestic partner living arrangement. What followed was the legalizing of infanticide and roughly sixty million innocent babies have been terminated so far. It hasn't been enough for America to be diabolical, but it is also guilty of funding other nations to do the same, such as Red China. No wonder America was accurately described in Revelation 17.5, as "The Mother of Harlots and of the Abominations of the Earth." Have you noticed how difficult it is to get justice anymore? This is truly the height of decadence!

It is no wonder then that God says to give Babylon a double judgment in Revelation 18.6-7. "Render to her just as she rendered to you and repay her double according to her works: in the cup which she mixed, mix double for her. In the measure that she glorified herself and lived luxuriously, in the same measure give her torment and sorrow; for she says in her heart, 'I sit as queen, and am no widow, and will not see sorrow.'"

It is evident, America's sins have been national in scope. In the past, God let the cup of iniquity get full before He brought judgment, but it looks like America's cup of iniquity is getting very full. <u>God's tolerance for sin does have a limit</u>, and He has been sending America wake-up calls, but few seem to be waking up. This is a concern because what follows are wake-up calls that will be much more intense. It needs to be understood that God would not be a God of love if He didn't at some point judge what is evil. When things go bad in a person's life he shouldn't blame God but the devil who caused the problem.

In Revelation 17.1 the angel says to John, "Come I will show you the judgment of the great harlot who sits on many waters, with whom the kings of the earth committed fornication, and the inhabitants of the earth were made drunk with the wine of her fornication".

Let's understand what is meant by the phrase, "…and the inhabitants of the earth were made drunk with the wine of her fornication." In the Greek, as mentioned before, the word "fornication" here means moral depravity and greed. This also means being less than honest and unethical to achieve one's aims.

Notice another section of that phrase, "...made drunk with the wine..." The wine here is being used as a bribe. What is it that would make other nations so willing and greedy to get from the U.S,? It is foreign aid and lots of it. This is the wine! In another place the words "filthy lucre" are used.

In 1 Timothy 3.3 and 3.8 the words "wine" and "filthy lucre" are both used in the same sentence (KJV). In other translations the word "money" is used for the word "lucre." With regard to the recipients of this wine, it has many different flavors or properties, such as bags of cash, most favored nation trading status, military hardware, millions deposited in secret Swiss bank accounts etc. So, what nation is most guilty to get nations to drink from this cup? Without a doubt, the United States is most prominent in this regard.

Back to Revelation 17.3 we see another ungodly trait observed. The verse says that the beast was full of names of blasphemy, What does the word "blasphemy" mean? It means words that revile God and anything that is religious. This is exactly what we are increasingly seeing in America today! Satanic forces are trying to purge America of anything which pertains to Christianity. They don't even want prayers to end in the name of Jesus.

So, in this verse we are seeing a spiritual analysis of the woman or America. She is choosing to be allied with Satan's desires for America rather than with God's desires for America. One-way deceptive change is coming about is through political correctness and the limiting of free speech. This is to prevent anything Christian from offending people of other faiths or of no faith.

Satan has introduced that which is diabolical very slowly into society, so people will gradually get used to it and then it becomes the norm. This keeps society from realizing how far it has declined from being a decent and moral people. For example, when I was going to college, we were told that the developing embryo in a woman that is pregnant is just a blob of tissue. That is a lie. The developing embryo has half the DNA of the mother and half the DNA of the father making it a fully human embryo. It also has its own heartbeat, fingerprints and blood type. It is not the mother's body but is its own person. So, an abortion even at the earliest stages terminates a human life. Proof of this is letting the fetus develop to full term and the mother **always** gives birth to a human baby.

Then there are those who are putting doubts in others minds about what gender they are. Jesus said in Mark 10.6, "From the beginning of creation God made them male and female." So what determines your gender? A male has an X and a Y chromosome, but a female has two X chromosomes. Does a biological test really need to be done to determine this? If one leaves their mind open to secular perversion they are courting undesired consequences. These on-going trends are fulfilling end-time Bible prophecy!

It appears what seals America's doom is allowing and sanctioning the killing of the saints. No other atrocious activity is mentioned after this in Revelation chapter seventeen. America is at war.

To see this, we go to Jeremiah 50.22-24 and see America, the policeman of the world (the hammer), being addressed. "A sound of battle is in the land and of great destruction. How the hammer of the whole earth has been cut apart and broken! How Babylon has become a desolation among the nations! I have laid a snare for you: you have indeed been trapped, O Babylon, and you were not aware; you have been found and also caught because you have contended against the Lord." The word "caught" means captured in the Hebrew. Again, this reveals America will come under occupation.

Now verse 28 confirms that we are not talking about Babylon under Belshazzar. "The voice of those who flee and escape from the land of Babylon declares in Zion the vengeance of the Lord our God, the vengeance of His temple."

When the Jewish people left Babylon under Cyrus they weren't fleeing or escaping. They were free to go. What we are actually seeing in this verse are Jews fleeing America because of the war and going to Zion or Israel, and declaring there, that this is God's judgment on America for the killing of His saints. Yes, the saints represent His temple (1 Corinthians 6.19; Ephesians 2.21).

Now there is more information in Scripture on how America is being destroyed. Jeremiah 51.1 says, "Thus says the Lord: Behold I will raise up against Babylon, against those who dwell in the midst of those who rise up against Me a destroying wind." In verse two what follows is the invasion of the land from all sides. From this passage what precedes the invasion of forces is a devasting nuclear strike where each nuclear blast destroys with a 600-mph wind, and this will kill millions of unsuspecting people. We saw confirmation of this previously in Isaiah chapter 47. In Revelation chapter eighteen it mentions three times that this destruction takes place in the span of one hour (v.10, 17, and 19). When I served aboard a fleet ballistic missile submarine, we had the capability to launch all 16 missiles in under an hour.

Governments know nuclear tipped missiles aren't cheap and they take a long time to produce so if they are going to use them, they will use them where they can do the most damage. Those targets will be large metropolitan areas and military bases.

If we understand the scripture is speaking about America being attacked with nuclear weapons, then we can also get a good idea of who the attackers are because there aren't very many countries that have these weapons and this capability. Russia and Red China will be at least two of the big aggressive nations involved here.

Some news sources has shown pictures of Chinese nationals crossing the southern border, males only, no family members and then they have vans waiting to bus them to other locations. Two known locations have been El Centro and the marine base in Camp Pendelton CA. Some recent reports are that marine sergeants are very upset that they are being forced to train these Chinese nationals. It has also been reported that ten thousand a month of these Chinese nationals have been coming across the border. It is independent news sources that have reported on this not the main stream news media.

CHAPTER EIGHTEEN

THE NEW JERUSALEM

At some time in the past you may have heard it taught that the new Jerusalem will come down from heaven upon the earth during the thousand year reign of Christ. There are a couple problems with this and its huge size applies to both of them. Revelation 21.16 says, "The city is laid out as a square; its length is as great as its breadth. And he measured the city with the reed: twelve thousand furlongs. Its length, breadth, and height are equal." Depending upon the Bible translation one reads twelve thousand furlongs is 1400 miles or 1500 miles long.

So, if you set down upon the earth a city that is 1500 miles long on each side, that area equals 2,250,000 square miles of city. The question is, where would you put it? The entire nation of Israel is only 7,849 square miles in size. If you set the city down on any of the inhabitable land area you would wipe out a number of nations in the process. Obviously, something is wrong with this picture here.

But then there is a second problem. Say you did find a place to put it; you wouldn't be able to get into it. Why not? Because of the curvature of the earth. To exaggerate a little to make a point, it would sit like trying to balance a book on a ball. The sides of the city would extend over the curvature of the land by seventy miles on all sides, and I don't know of anyone who can jump that far to get into one of the city gates.

Well, what if the city were only 1400 miles on a side; then you would only have to jump sixty miles to get in.

The point is, this earth just simply isn't big enough for a city of that size. The answer to this dilemma is found in Revelation 21.1. Verse one establishes the basis for the context we have been considering. "Now I saw a new heaven and a new earth for the first heaven and first earth had passed away..." Then in the second verse John sees the New Jerusalem coming down upon an entirely new earth. This tells us something about the new earth. It will be big enough to accommodate this huge city so that people will be able to get in the city gates. Therefore, the new earth will be considerably larger than our present earth.

Sometimes what isn't said provides additional information as well. With regard to this new earth, you don't hear God saying that He will take one of the planets He has already made to be the new earth. No, rather He says in Isaiah 65.17, "For behold, I create new heavens and a new earth..." The words imply it hasn't been done yet. This will be an entirely new creation from what we can now see in the heavens with our telescopes. We have not seen God perform a mighty act of creation like that before. Maybe He is going to put on a show for us.

AN ENIGMA

In Revelation 22.14-15 we observe what appears to be an enigma not well understood by many. It reads, "Blessed are those who do His commandments that they may have right to the tree of life and may enter through the gates into the city. But outside are dogs and sorcerers and sexually immoral and murderers and idolators and whoever loves and practices a lie."

Now here is the enigma. How can these ungodly people be outside the city of the New Jerusalem, which is on the new earth, if they were supposed to have been thrown into the lake of fire, after the great white throne judgment? The answer is found in what John meant by the use of the word "outside." This was a Christian term used by the early Church to mean "outside the faith." We have examples of that. Colossians 4.5 says, "Walk in wisdom toward those who are outside, redeeming the time." 1 Thessalonians 4.12 says, "that you may walk properly toward those who are outside…" And another reference can be found in 1 Timothy 3.7. So, John in Revelation 22 was just simply identifying who those are that are **"outside" the faith** that didn't make it, that didn't get translated to the new earth.

CHAPTER NINETEEN

THE FIRST AND SECOND CREATION

Does cosmic light determine the age of the earth? Scientists say the universe is 13.7 billion years old. The farthest known galaxy MAC0647-JD is 13.3 light years away, yet we see it. Therefore, it would need to be 13.3 billion years old in which it produced light so that light would have time to reach earth according to the theory. But the scientists also say the earth is only 4.54 billion years old.

The conclusion of the scientific data means the light from the furthest galaxies would already be inundating the earth's region with light when the earth came into existence. That means there is no light/age problem with regard to the age of the earth relative to the stars. It means the earth does not have to be old just because stars are far away. The distance the stars are from the earth does not determine the age of the earth.

Defaulting to the Word of God gives us a different picture of created objects with respect to the earth. When you incorporate the Supra-natural you might expect this. God says that after He created the heavens, He stretched them out. Isaiah 42.5 says, "Thus says God the Lord, who created the heavens and stretched them out…" Isaiah 45.12 says, "It is I who made the earth, and created man upon it. I stretched out the heavens with My hands and I ordained all their host."

So, if you have a central location of created luminaries and they are being spread apart from each other to great distances you don't then have to wait billions of years for light to reach you as the light is already at its initial point of origin before it begins moving away from you, and yet, you still see all the lights only they get smaller the farther away they go until, at some point, you then need a telescope to see many of them. God doesn't tell how fast He moved the luminaries apart only that He did it.

THE GAP THEORY.

What does it imply? It implies that when God spoke the earth into existence, He left this glob of material in the cosmos for billions of years before deciding to do something with it. It was therefore, a veritable wasteland for billions of years. Does the Bible address this? Yes, it does in Isaiah 45.18. It says, "For thus says the Lord, who created the heavens (He is the God who formed the earth and made it. He established it, and <u>did not create it a waste place</u>, but formed it to be inhabited), I am the Lord and there is none else." So, the verse reveals that at the time He was creating the earth He was visualizing the earth to be a habitable planet. Does it make any sense that God would want to delay His work for a few billion years before completing what He started?

It would seem we have the answer to that in Exodus 20.11. The verse reads, "For in six days the Lord made the heavens and the earth, the sea, and all that is in them, and rested on the seventh day." From this verse it doesn't look like He took any breaks until day seven.

No where in Scripture do we find God taking or requiring eons of time to do creative works. For example, when He made our sun and moon, He did it in just one day – <u>on day four</u> – and our sun is so big you could put one million, three hundred thousand earths inside the sun. We know that the beginning of creation week in which Adam was made only goes back a little over 6,000 years. Jesus, Himself, said "But from the <u>beginning of the creation</u> God made them male and female" (Mark 10.6).

Jesus indicated the creation was young. Therefore, in dating the sun scientists are off by over 4+ billion years. This reveals scientists have a real problem in establishing ages and frankly I would say they need to find out where they have erred. Why? Well, because God was there when everything was created and He gave His account of what He did to Moses who documented it. Our present-day scientists were not there!

It begs the question – who's account is most believable? If God can make our sun, a colossus of its size in one day, He certainly doesn't need eons of time to make the earth.

Isaiah 65.17-19 reveals, God, in the future, will do a new act of creation. It reads, "For behold I create new heavens and a new earth; and the former shall not be remembered or come to mind. But be glad and rejoice forever in what I create; for behold I create Jerusalem as a rejoicing and her people a joy. I will rejoice in Jerusalem and joy in My people; the voice of weeping shall no longer be heard in her, nor the voice of crying." So, did you notice who this new earth and new Jerusalem is created for? Yes, the verse said for God's people.

CHAPTER TWENTY

AMAZING ENCOUNTERS

I debated what the title of this chapter should be. When God chooses to use people for His purpose, He frequently chooses those you would least expect and I believe I fall into that category. What I value most is my relationship with the Lord and I am in that minority group of those who choose to believe what God has said, and that the Bible is true. Macro evolution just isn't believable!

My first notable encounter with the Lord came when I was eight years old. It was in the month of February on a Sunday night at church. That night I accepted the Lord as my Savior and became a born-again believer. When I rose from the altar I was a changed person. I couldn't get over how light I felt, and I felt such love for everyone and I wanted to tell people about Jesus. Little did I know that there would be another amazing encounter the following night.

The next night while sleeping I had a dream. In the dream I was taken up into heaven and I got to see Jesus. I saw first hand who He was that saved me. He wore a beautiful white robe. As He was walking toward me I also couldn't help noticing the Holy City a short distance away and the light of it just glistened with beauty. Heaven was similar to being on earth only everything there was perfect. The colors of everything you looked at were much more vivid than here on earth and there was no pollution of any kind. My time with the Lord was brief but an unforgettable amazing encounter. It was clear the Lord wanted me to cherish this new relationship with Him.

The next notable encounter came five years later when I was 13 years old. I had a real hunger for the things of God and it was after attending one of A.A. Allen's tent meetings that I heard there was going to be an all-night prayer meeting. I had never been to one of those before so I received permission from my parents to go to it. I managed with a great deal of effort, to stay awake and pray through the night. Little did I know that in the morning a blessing awaited me. I happened to look at my hands and on them was oil. This was no ordinary oil. It glistened and had the most wonderful fragrance; nothing like anything I'd ever experienced before. I began to realize, at that point, the Lord's anointing was on my life but it still wasn't apparent to me what He had in mind.

At the age of fifteen I became hooked on trying to understand Bible prophecy. It was then that I realized God was using it to confirm His Word.

Several more years went by and after completing military service I got married. The church we were attending was wanting more Sunday school teachers so I volunteered to teach an adult class on the book of Revelation. When I started, I did not have a developed outline for this class. That meant the lesson I would give the following Sunday was based on the preparation I did for it during the previous week.

There are two instances that stand out during this time of teaching. In my preparation time I came to the fifth trumpet judgment dealing with the locusts that would sting people and the pain would be so bad people would try and commit suicide but death would elude them and they wouldn't die. This mystified me in knowing how to relate this to the class in any meaningful way. So, I prayed about it asking the Lord to help the class to understand this. Well, the answer came that very week in the news. Someone in California tried to commit suicide by jumping off the Golden Gate bridge and they should have died only they didn't – they still lived.

One of the things that amazed me when at a later time I taught the Revelation class to a different group of adults I came to this same place in the study. In that same week of preparation another person jumped off the Golden Gate Bridge trying to commit suicide and also lived.

On a more personal level, I had another amazing experience. My morning routine was to arise from bed at 4:00 O'clock in the morning, shower, put on a robe and study for a couple of hours before going off to work. I had been receiving some amazing insight from the Lord in my preparation time. One morning as I was finishing up, I heard footsteps of someone in the house and I thought that was odd since my wife was still in bed and I hadn't got up from my chair yet. So, I went in to where she was and asked her if she heard anyone walking around and she said she hadn't. So, I just forgot about it until the next morning when at the close of my study session I heard footsteps again. This time I was more alert and I noticed the sound of those footsteps came from beside where I was sitting and began going across the room only this time, I could actually see the foot impressions being made in the carpet. Then I knew the Lord had been by my side aiding me in my study. Yes, another amazing encounter.

It was sometime after this that I completed two years at a community college plus two terms at the university that I felt the Lord was nudging me to enroll in Bible college. The Lord had a special way of getting my attention. It went something like this. I would go into the library to do my studying and all of a sudden, the Lord would deluge me with a sermon that would be so captivating that I couldn't concentrate on anything else. The Lord knew where my heart was and the secular university wasn't it.

It was now winter and I rented a large U-Haul trailer to pull behind our car. Our destination would change from Springfield Oregon to Springfield Missouri and it would occur in the dead of winter with our two small children. Our route would take us across Wyoming. There had been a lot of snow but the freeway had been cleared for the most part. The timing for our trip was remarkable as if we had started out two days earlier the highway would have been closed to travel. What hadn't been cleared though was access to rest areas and we needed to make a rest area stop. The snow was so deep it was difficult to tell where the road was and we were the only car to pull into it.

When we were ready to leave the rest area the car tires began slipping and the car started to slide sideways a little bit and I knew I would have to put on chains to have any chance of getting out of there. Suddenly two men appeared and asked if they could help us. This surprised me because I didn't know there was anyone else around and we were a long way from any town. In no time at all, they had put the chains on the car allowing us to get back on the road. When I turned around to thank them, they had disappeared. All I know is that the Lord provided help when we needed it. Yes, another amazing encounter.

It was my senior year in Bible college, and aside from my studies, Bible prophecy was still my passion. On this particular day I was in the middle of the living room floor with my books spread out around me making it easy to access lexicons, concordances, various Bible translations etc. All of a sudden, the room began filling with the presence of the Lord and His Spirit began to permeate every cell in my body. It was the most wonderful feeling I have ever felt. Along with that there was this most fragrant aroma that accompanied His presence and it was the exact same fragrance as when I had the oil on my hands years earlier.

Truly this was the Lord's anointing and I didn't want it to leave but I had no control over it and after a few minutes it lifted. Yes, another amazing encounter, and in none of these encounters was I praying to have any of these experiences. They just happened.

I will tell of one more instance in closing out this chapter. After I left Bible college we moved back to Springfield Oregon where I got a job in a hydraulic manufacturing plant. The Lord placed me here where I could be a witness for Him to people who would never darken the doors of a church. At this plant they made the parts that went into making hydraulic cylinders and my job was in inventory control where I collected the parts from the machines and kept them organized on shelves and then took them to fill orders for the assembly line where cylinders were then assembled.

Inventory control was located upstairs right over the machine shop which made the parts, and the machines were very noisy. I recognized that this was an ideal situation in which I could sing praise songs and choruses to the Lord and no one would hear me. So, that is what I did as I worked and this had been going on for many days. On this one day as I walked back to the order desk, all of a sudden I felt something whoosh past me and stand beside me brushing up against me. I couldn't visibly see who this was but I knew it had to be an angelic being because of what happened next. I got the feeling he interceded to protect me from unseen spiritual forces that were being arrayed against me because the next thing I knew it seemed those enemy forces were being repelled away from where I was with great force. At the same time, there was this pervasive heavenly aroma the exact same fragrance of the oil I experienced on my hands and in the house where I had been studying months earlier. Then this heavenly presence communicated with me not with words that anyone would hear but with thought telepathy concerning my future ministry.

Needless to say, I was so overwhelmed I was awestruck by this experience. About ten feet away were some other workers, and separating me from them was a high rack of parts they were using to fill orders for shipping. When I walked around to where they were, and when they took one look at me, they knew something had happened, and then all of a sudden they detected the same fragrance that was filling the upper room and they were speechless.

I did my best to explain to them what had happened. Well, the department leader hadn't been in the upper room when all this began happening and when he came upstairs the first thing he noticed was the heavenly aroma. At first, he didn't want to believe our explanation so he went back downstairs looking for women that might have walked into the shop overwhelming everyone with their perfume. He didn't find any. This department leader was a faithful Catholic. A short time later he and his family began attending a Four-Square church. That heavenly fragrance lasted for three days in the upper room before it finally dissipated.

CHAPTER TWENTY-ONE

A Proper Acknowledgement

Jesus makes the following statement in John 16.13. It reads, "However, when He the Spirit of truth, has come, He will guide you into all truth; for He will not speak on His own authority, but whatever He hears He will speak; and <u>He will tell you things to come</u>."

How do we view the Holy Spirit? With regard to the Holy Spirit a distinction needs to be made and clarified. There is a difference between the Person of the Holy Spirit and the gift of the Holy Spirit. When a person becomes a born-again Christian, at that moment, the Person of the Holy Spirit comes to dwell in them. They now have the Holy Spirit at that moment!

The Holy Spirit had not yet been given to Jesus' followers while He was with them, but He said, "And I will pray the Father, and He will give you another Helper, that He may abide with you forever – the Spirit of truth, whom the world cannot receive because it neither sees Him nor knows Him; but you know Him, for He dwells with you and will be <u>in you</u>" (John 14.16-17). So, when did Jesus send the Holy Spirit to be in them? It was at Pentecost.

Some would say that the scripture there (in Acts 2.4) says that they all spoke with other tongues. Yes, but one needs to see the larger picture. There are two parts to their initial experience. First of all, it says "they were all filled with the Holy Spirit" which fulfilled what Jesus said, that the Holy Spirit would be in them. It is only after they were filled that we see the 120 speak in other tongues. So, was it necessary for them to speak in other togues? Yes and no.

What is happening here is the birth of the Church and it was Jesus' intention for the Church to be comprised of Jews and Gentiles. So, the tongues were a <u>sign</u> to the Gentiles that the door had opened to them to be included with the Jewish people. Now it took a while for the disciples to get the message and this is why, for example, when Peter went to Cornelius home (a Gentile) that when the Holy Spirit fell on them, they also spoke in tongues (Acts 10.45-46) to <u>convince Peter and those with him</u> that God had accepted the Gentiles into the Church. It was not that tongues were required for one's salvation or even a required gift.

But this is how it should have been viewed, that the gift of speaking in other tongues was just that – <u>one of</u> the nine gifts of the Holy Spirit. In fact, in Acts 10.45 and Acts 11.17 this spiritual experience was described <u>as a gift</u> from the Holy Spirit.

When the apostle Paul was addressing the Corinthian church and the exercising of the spiritual gifts he makes the following comment, "…all do not speak with tongues do they?" (1 Corinthians 12.30).

This was an acknowledgement that not all believers had the gift of speaking in other tongues. Secondly, Paul further stated, "but earnestly desire the greater gifts" (1 Cor. 12.31). No where is there a scripture saying that you must have the gift of speaking in other tongues before you can receive any of the other gifts. So, if someone thinks you haven't arrived until you received the gift of tongues, I say you haven't arrived until you receive the greater gifts Paul said to seek after.

So, why was it important to include this last chapter? Because of the role the Holy Spirit plays in the translation of the saints. Ephesians 4.30 says, "And do not grieve the Holy Spirit of God, by whom you were sealed for the day of redemption.

www.ingramcontent.com/pod-product-compliance
Lightning Source LLC
LaVergne TN
LVHW061552070526
838199LV00077B/7012